Travel Egypt

Nile Cruise

Written and Researched By

Janet Wood

Travel Egypt Series on the Internet

www.travel-egypt.co.uk
www.ancientnile.co.uk

This book is dedicated to our nearest and dearest

Books in the Travel Egypt Series are; Nile Cruise (Paperback and eBook), Around Luxor (eBook), Photographing the Ancient Sites (eBook)

Websites: http://www.travel-egypt.co.uk & http://www.ancientnile.co.uk

You will find colour versions of the black and white photographs displayed in this book at: www.travel-egypt.co.uk/colour.php

Second Edition published in Great Britain March 21st 2011
© M J Wood Digital Media, Greater Manchester, England.

ISBN 978-0-9548049-6-1

Cover design and photo by Janet Wood

CONTENTS

INTRODUCTION

One of the questions I am regularly asked with regards to Egyptian travel is, 'What actually happens on an Egyptian Cruise?' So with this in mind I have written this book in order to go through what, in my experience, are the typical events of a Nile holiday. My intention is that hopefully by the time you have finished reading you will have a far better idea of what to expect so you can enjoy your holiday to the full. I hope it will prove an invaluable source of reference for you, both whilst preparing for your holiday and whilst you are away.

In order to ensure accuracy this book is based solely on my own personal experience and although I have written the book from the perspective of a UK traveller, over 99% of the information provided will be relevant to most tourists visiting Egypt. As well as covering the basic issues, I will also tell you, 'how it is', and not just romanticise the experience. Whilst this book contains information on the various sites regularly visited by the cruise ships, it is actually more concerned with general and practical information that you will be hard pressed to find elsewhere, especially in one place.

As each tour operator set its own agenda I can not guarantee to include all of the events that will be made available to you during your stay in Egypt, or that they will happen in the order I have indicated. For example one tour company may include a visit to 'The Workers Village' on the west bank and a Perfumery in Luxor, whilst another may choose Medinet Habu and a Papyrus Factory in Karnak. However, generally speaking, all the major sites I do mention should be covered at some stage during your holiday.

Whilst a Nile cruise may not give you a fully comprehensive look at Ancient Egypt, it does allow the visitor to get a taste of some of the best sites in a short time and at a budget price. Besides, if a Nile cruise was good enough for pharaoh, then a luxury cruise must surely be good enough for us mere mortals!

A typical Nile cruise ship
NOTE: You will find colour versions of all the photos in this book on our website: www.travel-egypt.co.uk/colour.php

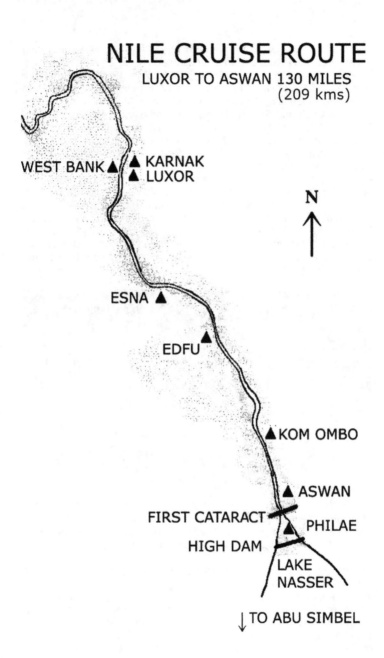

NILE CRUISE ROUTE

LUXOR TO ASWAN 130 MILES
(209 kms)

N

WEST BANK ▲   ▲ KARNAK
▲ LUXOR

ESNA ▲

EDFU ▲

▲ KOM OMBO

▲ ASWAN

FIRST CATARACT

PHILAE

HIGH DAM

LAKE
NASSER

↓ TO ABU SIMBEL

The British have been in love with Egypt and the Nile for a long time, ever since tourism was introduced by an adventurous man called Thomas Cook from Derbyshire who in 1869 organised the first tour of Egypt when he took a party of people from England to witness the opening of the Suez Canal. Then, later in 1872 the first 'Thomas Cook and Son' travel agency was established in Cairo and business began to flourish. By the late 1880s they began to lease steamers in order to reach the ancient sites in Upper Egypt and the famous cruising tours of Egypt became the enduring tourist attraction it still is today.

Unfortunately due to security reasons cruises from Cairo to Luxor are no longer available. There are a few cruises on Lake Nasser but these only visit the monuments in the old Nubian region, such as Abu Simbel. Therefore the most popular cruises by far start at Luxor, some 315 miles south of Cairo, and travel south to Aswan and it is for that reason I have concentrated on these. Besides, as Luxor houses over seventy percent of Egypt's ancient artefacts and sites, it's a very good place to start your voyage of discovery.

A land of biblical images

There are more than 300 ships cruising the Nile, many of which are five-star, offering trips of various durations including three, four or seven nights. Most of these 'Agatha Christie' style boats just seem to quietly slip through the landscape and are an excellent way of travelling the Nile.

As you leisurely cruise, the natural beauty of the river can take your breath away.

With the desert always in the background, life along the River Nile goes on much as it did in the days of the great Pharaohs, with villagers working the land, rearing livestock and fishing the river.

I could stare at the mostly unspoilt riverbank forever, imagining the life of the ancient Egyptians and a land bathed in legend and superstition.

6

As you travel you can't help but notice the proliferation of date palms that border the riverbanks. Dates have been a staple food in Egypt for thousands of years, possibly as early as 4000 BC. The dates are harvested in September. The Ancient Egyptians used the fruits to make date wine. Date palm leaves are still used for Palm Sunday celebrations in the Christian religion. In North Africa, they are commonly used for making huts. Mature leaves are also made into mats, screens, baskets, fans and their oil is suitable for use in soap and cosmetics.

A landscape of palms fringe the Theban Hills

Nile cruises are a mix of conducted tours, wholesome food, coddled relaxation, comfortable travel, fantastic sunsets and romantic scenery. So enjoy!

Many years ago a Nile cruise was my first introduction to Egypt and it whetted my appetite so much so that I couldn't wait to get back the following year to see the pyramids and 'Tutankhamun's treasures' at the Museum of Antiquities. Of course, you could always include a stay in Cairo as part of your Nile cruise package however your holiday will become more hectic and costly, involving extra accommodation and an internal air flight between Luxor and Cairo. One year I incorporated Cairo, Luxor and the Red Sea into a 10-day holiday, which proved very tiring. It's not too bad if you are fairly young and physically fit but the older you are, the more you will probably feel the pace.

You will find that there are many online travel companies who offer package holidays, tailor-made vacations, specialist tours, or all-inclusive stays. You can find Internet links to travel companies offering Egyptian holidays on our website at; www.travel-egypt.co.uk

The price of your holiday should include flights with meals, resort transfers, taxes, accommodation, around ten excursions and hopefully a free late checkout for your cabin. Child prices are usually only applicable when sharing with two full fare paying adults. Children are usually classed as 2-11 years old, however many cruises do not allow children under the age of twelve. Also note there will probably be an extra charge applied, around 2%, to the cost of your holiday if you book with a credit card, rather than a debit card. Baggage allowance varies between airlines but the norm is around 20kg (44 pounds) and 5kgs for hand luggage. (Take soft material hand luggage to keep the weight down.) Your included excursions should incorporate; Valley of the Kings, Colossi of Memnon, High Dam, The Unfinished Obelisk, the temples of Karnak, Luxor, Deir el Medina, Edfu, Kom-Ombo and Philae.

NILE HISTORY
In order to get a little understanding of the importance of the Nile we need to look first at its history. The river actually flows for some 4000 miles from its source in Rwanda to the Sea. In Egypt the length of the river from Aswan to Alexandria, where it flows into the Mediterranean, is some 560 miles (900km). The Nile has always been the backbone of Egypt and was crucial to the everyday life of the ancient Egyptians. Even their first calendar was based around it and drawn up long before the first dynasty, some 5000 years ago. The year had 360 days, with 5 god days. There were 3 seasons of 4 months with 3 weeks in each month and 10 days in each week. The year's seasons were named;
Akhet: Inundation (flood). July–October
Peret: Emergence out of the flood. November–February
Shemu: Time of drought. March–June

Counting the days of the year (left) and the gods representing the three seasons at Kom Ombo Temple

8

Without the Nile, and the annual inundation depositing rich silt to fertilise the valley, Ancient Egypt would never have come into being. This alluvial silt allowed the Egyptians to shrug off their desert nomadic lives and develop a strong agricultural society.

At the boundaries of the inundation the desert also acted as a natural defence against attack from other countries thereby isolating Egypt and allowing it to develop without outside influences.

The Nile, with both its advantages and disadvantages, moulded the way the ancient Egyptians lived and thought. Over thousands of years they learnt how to make the most of the river by harnessing and conserving the life-giving waters. They erected dykes, invented the shaduf, introduced irrigation, built broad reservoirs from earthen walls and dug canals in order to gain some control over the magnificent Nile and thereby increase the arable land available to them. It was this co-operation and organisation of its people, which ensured the growth of one of the earliest and greatest civilisations the world has ever seen.

The annual flooding happened during summertime and lasted until the end of October when the ground was left covered in a rich thick black soil, ideal for sowing crops like barley, flax and wheat. The earth was so fertile, that provided there was enough moisture left in the ground, it could produce two harvests a year. The ancient Egyptians even named their country 'Kemet' meaning 'Black Land'.

It was recorded that at the start of the flooding the clear waters would turn green with organic matter and it was during this period that the river was deemed 'unwholesome'. Next, the Nile water would turn a turbid red and very muddy, caused by the rains running over the red soil of the Abyssinian Mountains in Ethiopia. After this the waters would turn clear again. In readiness for these events the ancients would store a supply of clean water in jars until the Nile was once again safe to drink.

Structures known as Nilometers, usually in the shape of tunnels or wells, were used to measure the water levels of the River Nile for over 5000 years and are a notable reminder of Egypt's celebrated past.

Since the river has always been of critical economic importance to both ancient and modern civilizations alike, officials constantly gauged its water levels. In ancient times this was the job of Pharaoh's priests who also used the results to compute the levy of taxes payable by his subjects. A sufficient flooding heralded better crops and more taxes, whereas an insufficient flood meant the reverse.

As the Nile rose the Egyptians retreated with their livestock to their settlements on higher ground, which had been gradually formed by previous floods laying down heavy sands and gravels. Guards were also posted in order to monitor the dykes that were built to protect the cattle and villages.

Herodotus observed that when the Nile Valley was flooded, *'the whole country is converted into a sea and the towns, which alone remain above water, look like the islands in the Aegean'*. When the Nile inundation was exceptionally high, villages were frequently flooded which endangered lives, stock and property. Their vulnerable mud brick houses would become saturated by the water and collapse, sometimes inflicting heavy losses.

Nilometers at various points along the river monitored water levels
This one is at Edfu Temple

Pliny, a natural historian, assessed that a rise in the Nile waters exceeding sixteen cubits, or less than thirteen, would both result in famine. In other words too much water slowed up agriculture because the river receded too slowly and the sowing time was delayed because of the high moisture level in the soil. Whilst too little flooding meant there was not enough water for irrigation, therefore greatly reducing the region of arable land. (One cubit was the distance from the tip of the middle finger to the elbow – a length of 17–22 inches or 43-56 cm)

Pliny goes on to observe, *'A proper inundation is of sixteen cubits. Twelve cubits and the country suffers from famine and feels a deficiency even at thirteen. Fourteen causes joy, fifteen security, sixteen delight, and at seventeen, panic'*. It was a very fine balance!

As the agriculture of Egypt revolved around the Nile, so did the social life of its population. During inundation, when there was little to do, people had more time for recreational activities. They played games, held sporting tournaments such as wrestling, gymnastics, bull fighting, and regularly feasted. But not everything was fun and games, as it was also during this period that Pharaoh would find work for the idle hands of his subjects by conscripting them into his various construction projects. However, the evidence so far seems to suggest that his people did not object to this, as they were paid well with food and drink rations.

When the Nile receded the appearance of the land had radically changed and there was a great rush to restore boundaries. There would be many disputes over land ownership as markers had moved, banks had collapsed, and distinguishable features had disappeared. Many of these disputes ended up in court. To help regulate this problem a group of officials known as 'cord stretchers' worked on such problems. These men were the ancestors of our modern surveyors and one of the reasons why the Egyptians invented geometry.

As their natural highway, the Nile was also the chief means of transport, making roads superfluous, except between close villages. Virtually everything moved by boat; people, animals and goods. Officials, tax collectors, priests, peasants, landowners, pharaohs, all did their business via the Nile. Most of the boats were not heavy, seagoing vessels, but transport barges or simple sailing boats. Some large wooden boats were built from Lebanon cedar, but these were mainly used for special ceremonies.

Simple reed boat used to navigate the Nile in ancient times

After death Pharaoh even took his final journey via the Nile as his body encased in a magnificent sarcophagus was ferried across the water from the east side to the 'Land of the Dead' on the west bank for burial.

Probably one of the heaviest cargos ever to be transported on the Nile was the enormous granite obelisks that were erected on ancient sites along the Nile. The tallest obelisk left standing in Egypt is Queen Hatshepsut red granite obelisk at Karnak which weighs over 300 tons and has a height of approximately 30 meters. The obelisk would have been shipped by boat from the quarries at Aswan to Luxor a distance of some 300 miles. Just how they managed to get such a huge structure on and off a boat without modern day lifting equipment seems incredulous.

The Nile is the only major river to flow south to north - most flow the opposite way. Nile boats therefore sailed south with the wind and drifted north with the current. The ancient Egyptian word to sail meant 'to go south' and downstream meant, 'to go north'.

Harbours were not necessary on the Nile as boats could easily tie up at the riverbank.

For the most part the Egyptian Nile is a gentle moving river and during the time of the ancients it would have been crammed with fish. Its easy flowing current made fishing very popular and ancient Egyptians used hooks, nets and baskets to catch the fish. Everyone enjoyed fishing, from the young to old, peasant to noble. Fishing took place on the river, within its marshlands, lakes, canals, tributaries and even ponds, which the richer landowners created on their estates. Fishing was both a pleasurable sport and an important source of food. The marshlands also provided good areas for bird hunting, as the Nile lay on the route of many migratory birds.

These obelisks were carried over 300 miles on the River Nile before being erected at Karnak. A tremendous feat.

Game would be tracked down in a flat reed boat, which could slip silently through the thickets on the marshes where the water birds lived. Pharaohs are often depicted in tomb and temple reliefs holding various weapons such as spear, club, or bow and arrow as they hunted in the delta region. For most of the population the Nile provided the bulk of the protein in their diet.

The Nile also played a pivotal role in Ancient Egyptian religion as according to their beliefs when the soul of a deceased reached the River Nile they had to correctly answer a series of questions and recite from a papyrus before the ferryman of a magical boat agreed to transport them across the Nile to the kingdom of Osiris and 'Life after Death'.

Fishing is still very important to villagers

The Egyptians also believed that the Nile was the centre of the world and that the place from which it originated was 'the beginning of the world'. The creation describes how a muddy island rose out of the 'primordial ocean', a scenario which they saw re-enacted every year towards the end of inundation, further reinforcing their conviction.

The Egyptians would annually celebrate the inundation with a great festival on the 'Night of the Clouds' (*Gerekh en Haty*), which heralded the beginning of the flood. Surprisingly, the ancient Egyptians did not view the river as a god and '*Haapi*' the river deity, was regarded more as a 'Spirit of the Nile'. According to legend the flood was the arrival of Haapi from a cavern at Aswan from where he discharged the rising waters. Because of this the ancient Egyptians orientated themselves towards the south and the mythological source of the Nile. An alternative explanation given for the inundation was that the floodwaters were the tears of the goddess Isis as she wept for the loss of her beloved husband, Osiris, slain at the hand of his evil brother, Seth.

The ancient Egyptians never discovered the true source of the River Nile and simply called it, *itrw*, 'the river'. At times it was even referred to as the sea. It's believed the word Nile is derived from the Greek word *Nelios*, meaning river valley.

Every year the ancient Egyptians watched their land disappear, only to see it re-emerge as new fertile land. This cycle of death and rebirth shaped their character, their gods, and the understanding of their existence in relationship to life and the cosmos.

In the area of the Nile Delta in Lower Egypt, the river splits into two great branches, the western and eastern, known respectively as the Rosetta and Damietta arms. The area between these two, gave birth to many major cult centres, notably Memphis, Tanis and Sais that were dedicated to gods such as Bastet, Osiris, Buto, Ra, and Horus.

Along its route, the ancient Egyptians diverted the waters of the River Nile where necessary, enabling an intricate network of canals and waterways that would irrigate the land and serve the important towns, temples and sacred complexes, such as the pyramids at Giza, Medinet Habu and Deir el Medina.

The River Nile was the fundamental provider of a great nation which was totally nurtured and defined by its bounty. The ancients utilised every aspect of the river and their achievements down the ages deserves both recognition and praise. Of all the world's great rivers the Nile blessed its people with the most reliable and predictable cycle of seasons. It provided transport, recreation, vegetation, food and clean drinking water for the entire country. Today the Aswan dam may have curtailed the annual flood but the Nile is no less important than it was two thousand years ago. As the Greek Historian Herodotus once famously penned two and a half thousand years ago, 'Egypt is the gift of the Nile'.

Children frolicking in the Nile

Large granite boulders at the 1st Cataract at Aswan showing water levels

ON ARRIVAL

Flights from the UK to Luxor take approximately five hours. Regarding the US, some flights do fly direct to Egypt, whilst others fly via a European stop-off, such as London or Frankfurt. You will need to check at the time of booking, but an average time is 28-32 hours.

Tourist visas for Egypt can be obtained upon arrival in Egypt for citizens of most countries, including the UK. You will also need a passport that is valid for at least six months and with at least one blank page. If you are 16 or over and do not yet have a passport of your own it is recommended that you apply for one at least six weeks before your holiday. As you enter the terminal you will be handed a visa form, which you will need to complete with your name, address, age, passport, country, flight number etc. The visa will then be checked and stamped, usually at the Bureau de Change counter. The present 30-day tourist visa costs £10 (15US$) and normally they ask that you pay with your national currency, i.e. UK Sterling, US dollars, Australian dollars. This is because Egypt is a relatively closed economy, which means they limit the amount of Egyptian currency you can bring into the country but there are no restrictions on the amount of 'foreign' currency you can take in.

A word of warning a representative for your travel company may already possess visa stamps that he will stick into your passport for you which you later pay him for. Although perfectly aboveboard what they don't tell you is that they will charge you extra for the service, which was £3 per person above the going rate last time I visited. You will also need to complete an entry card, which will be checked by passport control. Your passport will then be stamped.

I have included a money conversion chart in the final section of this book for GBP, USD, CAD, EURO and AUD currencies, however as the exchange rate constantly changes you should use this only as a rough guide. I would suggest that you check the current exchange rate just before you leave for your holiday and add your own up-to-date chart on the blank page at the end of the book. The currency in Egypt is Egyptian pounds, expressed locally as LE, which stands for 'livre égyptienne'. There are 100 piastres in one Egyptian pound.

After passing through passport control and collecting your luggage, a coach will transport you to your Nile cruise ship. This should take approximately 20 minutes.

You may find that some of the airport staff and locals try to relieve you of money as you're being checked through the airport, usually after they have just flattered you regarding the beauty of your partner. Do not be taken in by this (even though your partner is beautiful ☺) and politely refuse to hand over any money. By the end of your holiday this will have become second nature to you!

If you want to use a luggage trolley you will be charged 2 Egyptian pounds for the privilege. If your bags are not too heavy, or better still have wheels, I would strongly suggest that you do not bother as the coaches are usually parked just outside the main doors, a distance of some 100 yards.

There will also be a number of unofficial luggage handlers waiting outside, eager to carry your bags to the coach, even to the point of trying to grab them from your hand in their eagerness to 'earn' a fee. If you do not want their help, be firm and say, no (La), whilst shaking your head. If you do use their service expect to pay 2LE. If you have no Egyptian money, you can offer sterling, but they will expect at least a £1 coin (10LE). A word of warning, do not expect to be given change if you don't have the correct money.

In one instance I saw a fellow tourist offer a 20p UK coin (2LE) to one Egyptian who had more or less snatched the bag from his hand and carried it a mere 20 yards. However this was angrily dismissed and a demand for more money issued. When the man refused a heated debate ensued with more Egyptians joining in, until the travel representative intervened and the disgruntled Egyptians moved on to their next victim. Once you find your coach your bags will be loaded onto the vehicle by the driver. Again you will probably be pestered for a tip, but it isn't necessary as your travel company is already paying for his services. Just ignore his demands as if you haven't noticed and board the coach. The journey to your cruise ship will take approximately 20 minutes during which time your travel rep will give you a quick cursory pep talk and cite a couple of points of interest on the way.

Once aboard the boat you will most likely be asked to hand in your passports as part of the Egyptian security measures, this will be returned to you anytime between a couple of hours or the end of the week. Your travel representative will advise. Your luggage will be brought to your cabin by a member staff and again he will expect a tip. I usually give them 2LE.

Depending upon your time of arrival, you will be asked to join your rep's welcoming meeting either that day, or the following morning. I strongly suggest that you do attend as you will be given information about the itinerary, boat amenities, plus the opportunity to book additional excursions that aren't part of your holiday package. These will be presented quite enthusiastically as the travel reps are usually on commission; however this is not to say they are not good value for money. If this is your first visit to Egypt then I would suggest you consider booking a couple of them. By far the most popular extra excursions taken are;

ABU SIMBEL (I will talk about this in more detail later)

BALLOON FLIGHT OVER THE WEST BANK
If you can afford it and don't mind heights than a balloon flight is another great way of seeing the antiquity sites of the west bank. If

the weather is clear and there isn't too much wind then you will have a fabulous trip. Seeing the 'open museum' below as you drift over the Theban hills is quite something. The trip will probably also include breakfast in the desert. However be warned it is a very early start, around 4.30am. Because of new restrictions availability is limited so make sure you book early. Also ensure that you are covered by insurance for the flight.

DAY TRIP TO CAIRO
If you think it's unlikely that you will ever return to Egypt then I would definitely recommend this trip which includes a visit to the pyramids, sphinx, followed by lunch, and then on to the Cairo Museum of Antiquities where the treasures of Tutankhamun and the royal mummies are housed. However it doesn't come cheap as it involves a plane flight. You will be able to photograph any exteriors but no interiors such as the inside of the pyramids and museum. The day starts around 3.30am!

SOUND AND LIGHT SHOW AT KARNAK
The narration gives a historical introduction of the great city of Thebes, the erection of Karnak temple and the glorious achievements of some great Pharaohs. The show begins as you walk along the Avenue of Sphinx, before passing through the towering 1st pylon (gateway) and into the Great Court. As you walk through the temple a loud commentary, imitating Pharaoh's voice, narrates the history of Upper Egypt as lights illuminate various sections of the temple against the night sky, showcasing the achievements of rulers such as King Tutankhamun, Ramses II and Queen Hatshepsut.
The second part of the Sound and Light Show finds spectators seated overlooking the sacred lake as you listen through speakers on either side to a description of the great legacy of Karnak. As the sound resonates back and forth across the water, you look towards the illuminated temple as the story of Egypt continues.
Whilst the show is suitable for all ages the complex is very dark and the loud commentary may frighten young children. Also many youngsters may become bored.
Is the show value for money? Afraid the jury is out on this one. If you have an interest in ancient Egyptian history and you are able to let your imagination work for you, then you will enjoy the show. Others however will say it was boring. Personally I do consider them to be quite unique with the night experience adding a different air of mystery to the ruins that you can't fully appreciate during the day. You will be given the opportunity to see a similar show at Philae Temple, near Aswan but once you've seen one, there is no need to see another. Of the two I would recommend the Karnak show for the reason given in the tip below. The show lasts approximately 60 minutes and there are three shows in different languages at different times on different days. (See table)

TIP: The ground at Karnak is uneven and dusty so wear comfortable flat walking shoes. TIP: If you feel confident enough I suggest the Karnak Sound and Light Show is one trip you could easily organise yourself and save money. Admission is 100LE per person and you should buy your ticket from the entrance at least thirty minutes before the start of the show. A return taxi shouldn't cost you anymore than 50LE (probably a lot less – around 30LE if you've honed your negotiation skills) – but you will need to haggle with the taxi driver and don't pay him until the return journey. Depending upon your ship's mooring, in many cases you may even be close enough to walk to the temple. Last year our ship was docked directly opposite Karnak, a matter of a two minutes walk.

Therefore the total maximum cost for two persons would be 250LE (£26), compared to £50 via your tour company, a saving of £24! Find out which day your tour guide is planning their visit and then travel independently to the same show.

SOUND AND LIGHT SHOWS AT KARNAK

DAY	1st show	2nd show	3rd show
Sunday	German	English	Italian
Monday	English	French	Spanish
Tuesday	Japanese	English	By Booking
Wednesday	German	English	French
Thursday	English	French	Arabic
Friday	English	French	By Booking
Saturday	French	English	German
Winter: Oct-Apr	6:30 P.M.	7:45 P.M.	9.00 P.M.
Summer: May-Sept	8:00 P.M.	9:15 P.M.	10:30 P.M.

*Times, prices and shows are subject to change. Always check locally.

ADDITIONAL EXCURSIONS: I have included a list below which details various additional excursions with their prices in sterling. These prices may vary from company to company and should only be used as a guide when budgeting for your holiday.

Excursions	Adult Price	Child Price
Abu Simbel via bus	£80	£45
Abu Simbel by plane	£180	£135
Balloon Flight	£90	£45
Tour of Luxor	£15	£10
Nubian Village	£25	£15
Sound & Light Philae	£25	£20
Sound & Light Karnak	£25	£20

Cairo Visit	£285	£210
Tour of Aswan	£45	£25
Nubian Village	£25	£15

*Prices are subject to change. Always check locally.

Payment can usually be made in Sterling, Euros, Dollars, Visa, MasterCard, Egyptian pounds or travellers cheques. You will probably find that no refunds are given whatsoever with less than 48 hours notice and none given at all for excursions that include flights, boat or train bookings. Child prices are usually 2-11 years, with 12 plus being charged adult prices.

Hot air balloon landing on the West bank

19

PHARONIC RULERS FROM 1551 BC to 30 AD

Period and Dynasty	Reign BC	Years Ruled

NEW KINGDOM DYNASTY

This era was a golden time for Egypt, a period that was rich with extraordinary Pharaohs such as Ahmose, Hatshepsut, Tuthmoses III, Akhenaten, Nefertiti, Tutankhamun and Ramses II. It was a time when the country's civilization was at its peak.

Period and Dynasty	Reign BC	Years Ruled
DYNASTY XVIII (18)		
Ahmose	1550-1525	25 years
Amenhotep I	1525-1504	21 years
Tuthmoses I	1504-1492	12 years
Tuthmoses II	1492-1479	13 years
Queen Hatshepsut	1479-1457	22 years
Tuthmoses III	1479-1425	54 years
Amenhotep II	1428-1397	31 years
Tuthmoses IV	1397-1388	9 years
Amenhotep III	1388-1351	37 years
Akhenaten (Thebes and Amarna)	1351-1334	17 years
Smenkare	1337-1333	4 years
Tutankhamun	1333-1323	10 years
Ay	1323-1319	4 years
Horemheb	1319-1292	27 years
DYNASTY XIX (19)		
Ramses (Ramesses) I	1292-1290	2 years
Sety I	1290-1279	11 years
Ramses II (The Great)	1279-1213	66 years
Merenptah	1213-1203	10 years
Amenmesses	1203-1200	3 years
Sety II	1200-1194	6 years
Merenptah-Siptah	1194-1185	9 years
Queen Twosret	1185-1186	9 years
DYNASTY XX (20)		
Setnakhte	1186-1182	4 years
Ramses III	1182-1151	31 years
Ramses IV	1151-1145	6 years
Ramses V	1145-1142	3 years
Ramses VI	1142-1134	8 years
Ramses VII	1134-1126	8 years
Ramses VIII	1126-1125	1 year
Ramses IX	1125-1107	18 years
Ramses X	1107-1103	4 years
Ramses XI	1103-1070	33 years

THIRD INTERMEDIATE PERIOD

This was a period of fractured kingship, with Egypt in decline and turmoil. Pharaohs ruled at Tanis in the Delta region (North), whilst the ever increasingly powerful High Priests of Amun ruled Upper (Southern) Egypt from Thebes. The country was reunited for over a century in the 22nd Dynasty but by 850 BC the country was again in turmoil with the kingdom quickly fragmenting with much infighting for dominance in Upper and Lower Egypt, hence two rulers at different centres.

DYNASTY XXI (21)

At Tanis

Smendes	1070-1044	26 years
Amenemnesut	1044-1040	4 years
Psusennes I	1044- 993	47 years
Amenemope	996 - 984	52 years
Osochor	984 - 978	6 years
Siamun	978 - 959	19 years
Psusennes II	959 – 945	14 years

At Thebes

Piankh	1070-1068	3 years
Pinudjem I	1068-1032	30 years
Masaharti	1032-1013	19 years
Menkheperre	1013- 988	25 years
Smendes II	988- 987	1 year
Pinudjem II	987- 969	18 years
Psusennes II	959- 945	14 years

DYNASTY XXII (22)

Lower Egypt

Shoshenq I	945-924	31 years
Osorkon I	924-889	35 years
Takeloth I	889-877	12 years
Shosheng II	877-875	3 years
Osorkon II	875-837	38 years
Shosheng III	837-798	39 years
Shosheng III (a)	798-785	13 years
Pimay	785-774	11 years
Shosheny V	774-736	38 years

Upper Egypt

Harsiese	870-850	20 years
Takeloth II	841-816	25 years
Pedubastis I	830-805	25 years
Osorkon IV	730-715	15 years

DYNASTY XXIII (23)

Meremum	818-793	25 years

Iuput I	804-783	21 years
Shoshenq IV	783-777	6 years
Osorkon III	777-749	28 years
Takeloth III	754-734	20 years
Rudamun	734-731	3 years
Iuput II	731-720	11 years
DYNASTY XXIV (24)		
Tefnakhte	728-720	8 years
Shoshenq VI	720-715	5 years
Bekenranef	720-715	5 years

LATE DYNASTIC PERIOD

During this time there were several foreign rulers of Egypt including Nubian and Persian, who took advantage of Egypt's weakened state. There was a time of prosperity in the 26th Dynasty but Egypt was conquered by Persia during the 27th Dynasty before regaining independence during the 29th Dynasty.

DYNASTY XXV (25) (Nubian rule)		
Kashta	760-748	12 years
Piya	748-716	32 years
Shabaka	716-702	14 years
Shabitku	702-690	12 years
Taharqa	690-664	26 years
Tantamani	664-656	8 years
DYNASTY XXVI (26)		
Psammeticus I	664-610	54 years
Necho I	610-595	15 years
Psammeticus II	595-589	6 years
Apries	589-570	19 years
Amasis	570-526	44 years
Psammeticus III	526-525	1 year
DYNASTY XXVII (27)		
Cambyses (Persian)	525-522	3 years
Darius I	522-486	36 years
Xerxes	486-465	21 years
Artaxerxes I	465-424	41 years
Darius II	424-405	19 years
Artaxerxes II	405-401	4 years
DYNASTY XXVIII (28)		
Amyrtaios	404-399	5 years
DYNASTY XXIX (29)		
Nepherites I	399-393	6 years

Pshenmut	393-393	<1 year
Achoris	393-380	13 years
Nepherites II	380-380	<1 year
DYNASTY XXX (30)		
Nectanebo I	380-362	18 years
Teos	365-360	5 years
Nectanebo II	360-343	17 years

PERSIAN KINGS

Egypt once again becomes a Persian Province.

Artaxerxes III	343-338	5 years
Arses	338-336	2 years
Darius III	335-332	3 years

MACEDONIAN KINGS

Alexander the Great conquered Egypt in 332 BC and so began the 300 year Hellenistic (Greek) period.

Alexander the Great	332-323	9 years
Philip Arrhidaeus	323-316	7 years
Alexander IV	316-304	12 years

THE PTOLEMIES

Ptolemy I	304-284	20 years
Ptolemy II	285-246	39 years
Ptolemy III	246-221	25 years
Ptolemy IV	221-205	16 years
Ptolemy V	205-180	25 years
Ptolemy VI	180-145	35 years
Ptolemy VII	145-145	<1 year
Ptolemy VIII	145-116	29 years
Joint rulers:		
Ptolemy IX, X, XI & Cleopatra III	116-80	36 years
Ptolemy XII	80-58	22 years
Berenice IV	58-55	3 years
Ptolemy XII (again)	55-51	4 years
Ptolemy XIII (jointly)	51-47	4 years
Cleopatra VII (jointly)	51-30	21 years
Ptolemy XIV (jointly)	47-44	3 years
Ptolemy XV (jointly)	44-30	14 years

Please note: Where dates are subject to debate I have used the most popular consensus. These dynasties cover the building of the main sites you will visit on your cruise, especially the New Kingdom and Ptolemy periods.

ITINERARY

DAY ONE

Your first morning will begin around 7.30 am, when you will most likely cross over to the West Bank of the River Nile on the first of your excursions. Here, in the ancient area known as the 'Theban Necropolis' you will find the tombs and mortuary temples of the New Kingdom pharaohs.

TOMBS: Tombs were the final resting place of the pharaoh and were the vessel by which he entered the next world. Originally pyramids were used but by the New Kingdom period the idea of pyramid tombs was abandoned, with cost and robberies being the principal reasons. Some of the tombs were also built for queens, princes, princesses and nobles.

MORTUARY TEMPLES: Unlike temples which were dedicated to the gods, Mortuary temples were always for royalty and built by the pharaohs for the worship of themselves, whether living or dead. The ritual in all mortuary temples was very similar and included the processional carrying of a statue of the king into the temple where food, drink, incense, flowers, prayers and chants would be offered to his highness. The only difference was in the number of priests and offerings that took part in the ceremonies, for it was noted that when a new dynasty began then attendance of earlier mortuary temples were apt to suffer from dwindling numbers as the new king's mortuary temple took precedence.

The travel company provides guides for all the tours and you will probably be split into groups of about twenty. Quite often the guides are in their final year at university where they are studying Egyptology or Archaeology and are usually very informative and quite witty. However, you may sometimes have a little trouble understanding their accent.

Preparation is key to all your trips and none more so, than the Valley of the Kings where you personally choose three tombs to visit. I have listed a few examples below and your guide will probably make their own suggestions but neither should be a substitute for reading up on all the tombs before you leave so you can make an informed decision as to the ones you think will be the most interesting. Have more than three choices ready as the tombs which are open to the general public do change.

The trip to the Necropolis will last approximately four to five hours.

COLOSSI OF MEMNON

Your first stop will probably be to the huge statues known as the Colossi of Memnon. For the past 3400 years (since 1350 BC) they have stood in the Theban Necropolis and originally flanked the entrance to the grand temple of Amenhotep III.

Each statue represents king Amenhotep III seated on his throne, wearing the Nemes (royal headdress) while the divine cobra is protecting his forehead. Two shorter figures carved into the front of his throne alongside his legs are his wife Tiye and mother Mutemwiya. On the sides of the colossi there are representations of the Nile god Haapi with lotus and papyrus plants, symbolizing the union of Upper and Lower Egypt. The original function of the Colossi was to stand guard at the entrance to Amenhotep's memorial temple, of which very little remains.

The statues are made from blocks of quartzite sandstone and were transported some 675 km (420 miles) from quarries near Cairo to Thebes (modern day Luxor). Both figures are in poor condition with the features above the waist virtually unrecognizable. During a 27 BC earthquake the statues were damaged and became known for a bell like tone that usually occurred in the morning due to rising temperatures and humidity. According to legend hearing the 'Vocal Memnon' would bring you luck and the reputation of the statue's powers travelled the length of the known world bringing a stream of visitors to the area, including several Roman Emperors.

Unfortunately restoration work that was carried out during the time of the Roman Emperor Septemius Severus forever cured the statues of their 'singing'. The name Memnon, means 'Ruler of the Dawn', and was probably named so because of the ringing sound.

You can photograph and video the statues.

One of the Colossi

25

MUMMIFICATION PROCESS

Before I talk about the Valley of The Kings you may be interested in the history of mummification.

The first mummies in Egypt were preserved naturally when the deceased was buried in the desert sands and desiccation (drying out) took place. Bodily fluids would seep into the sand and what remained namely; skin, hair, tendons and ligaments would dry naturally.

The ancient Egyptians believed that to enjoy the Afterlife, the body of the deceased should bear as close a resemblance to the living person as possible. Features of the face were often modelled in linen bandages and painted. Even nipples and the male sex organs have been found modelled in cloth and placed in position so the deceased would be entire in the afterlife.

Canopic jars. Used to store the mummy's organs

When graves became more elaborate and the deceased were no longer just buried in the desert, the ancient Egyptians found that bodies started to decay, creating the complete opposite to what they strived for. So they started to look for ways to emulate the preserving properties of the sand graves by artificial means.

By the First Dynasty there was evidence that natron, a natural salt found in Egypt, was being used. The body would be covered in the salt, which acted like the hot desert sand and started the process of desiccation. However using natron alone proved not to be enough, as bodies would still decompose from the inside out, due to the moisture left in the internal organs.

Evisceration (disembowelling) was the next stage in the development of mummification, which involved removing the internal organs so the moisture they contained did not cause internal rotting of the corpse. Removal of the brain was done through the nose, using a hooked pick which liquefied it. The heart was treated and then put back in place as the Egyptians believe it housed the deceased's soul. Other organs such as the liver and lungs would be wrapped in linen, coated in resin and laid close to the corpse, either in a recess, or in later dynastic periods, in canopic jars. This was to ensure that the deceased would still be whole in the afterlife.

The entire body was then covered in many layers of linen, which were impregnated with resin to try and keep out external elements. The quality of the linen used to wrap the mummy varied according to the quality of the mummification. Reams and reams of bandages were used to give shape to the dried out corpse.

It's believed that the word 'mummy' comes from the Arabic word 'mummiya' meaning bitumen - a tar-like substance. This is because when early Arabs saw mummies covered in black resin, they thought that the ancients had used bitumen.

Immortality depended entirely upon the mummification of the body, as the process also preserved the 'Ka', the spirit that accompanied the physical body in life. If the body decayed, then so did the 'Ka'.

The New Kingdom mummies in the Valley of the Kings (18-20th Dynasties) are some of the best-preserved mummies in the world, demonstrating how skilful the priests had become at perfecting the process.

VALLEY OF THE KINGS

Photography in the Valley of the Kings is no longer permitted and all camera and video equipment have to be handed in at the entrance or left in your coach. (I suggest you do the latter) You can't take any bags in with you and have to pass through a metal detector before entering the new entrance building. Talk about over the top!

Maybe there is some justification for stopping internal photography of the tombs, as people were constantly using flash, even though clearly instructed not to, but to stop external photography is, in my opinion, totally ridiculous. Then, just to rub salt into the wound, when you actually get into the valley you are constantly bombarded by locals trying to sell you photos, postcards and other literature. If the touts were restricted to one area, ok, but they are literally everywhere and present an unremitting pestering, which frankly I found extremely annoying, as did many others tourists. I believe their presence in the valley should be stopped and relegated to a specific area as they are thoroughly spoiling the experience for many visitors.

Your tour guide may recommend you purchase a pack of twenty 8x6 photographs from the official photographer for 50LE. If you do want some decent photos I suggest you go with these and not the other junk being peddled by the local touts. Obviously they are dearer but far better quality, although sadly, they won't make up for you not having a personal photo of yourself stood in front of Tutankhamun's tomb. I believe the Supreme Council of Antiquities has gone way overboard with their current photographic restrictions, not only in the Valley of the Kings, but in the museums and interior of Abu Simbel. I can still hear the constant complaints from fellow tourists ringing in my ears.

From the coach you pass through the new visitors centre and its model of the valley. You will also find public toilets here. If you want toilet roll you will be charged 1LE for it! I keep a supply of tissues in my bag or pocket as I refuse to pay for such a basic necessity.

The ticket kiosk is just outside of the centre to the right, but as your visit should be included in your holiday your guide will purchase all tickets for the group. A motorised train will take you to the main site and from here your guide will escort you through the main thoroughfare.

Tour guides are no longer allowed to speak in the tombs so the vast majority will give a brief outline of the valley and its history before recommending several of their favourite tombs and leaving you to your own devices. Your ticket will allow you to visit three tombs.

There is a two-tiered cafeteria and rest area with fans on the ceiling where you can take shade and purchase drinks but at a very exorbitant price. A can of coke last year was 45LE! Your tour guide will probably arrange to meet you around this area after giving you an hour or so to complete your visit. It can get unbearably hot in the valley so carry plenty of water. I also carry a hand-held fan for the humid tombs.

HISTORY OF THE VALLEY

Pharaohs of the New Kingdom period believed that the Valley of the Kings was the ideal burial ground since the dominant peak had a pyramidal shape and the valley had only one entrance, which could easily be guarded by the special elite tomb police, the 'Medjay'.

For a period of nearly 500 years tombs were constructed in the area for each pharaoh, with Tuthmoses I thought to be the first king to be buried there.

The valley stands on the west bank of the Nile, opposite modern-day Luxor, within the heart of the Theban Necropolis and is known to contain 63 tombs and chambers. It was the principal burial place for all the major royal figures of the Egyptian New Kingdom, together with those of a number of privileged nobles.

The naturally occurring geological pyramid at the Valley of the Kings

The construction of pharaoh's tomb was started at the time of his coronation and continued until their death. If he died soon after coming to power than his tomb would be small, likewise if his reign was long then his tomb would be huge, as was the case of Ramses II.

From the time of pharaoh's death there would be seventy days in which to finish the tomb, with cutters, plasterers, painters, and inspectors etc all rushing to complete on time.

The vast majority of royal tombs are decorated with scenes from Egyptian mythology and give clues to the beliefs and funerary rituals of the period. Many of the tomb walls and roofs are covered with hieroglyphs, deities, and painted with a profusion of colours that have survived for thousands of years and you can't help but be captivated by the beauty and quality of the illustrations.

Ancient Egyptians believed colour was an essential part of life and their palette had six colours; red, green, blue, yellow, black and white. Red was the colour of power and victory, as well as fury and inferno. Green was the colour of fertility, growth and new life. Blue was the colour of water, heaven, creation and the cosmos. Yellow (or gold) was the colour of the indestructible and eternal, such as the gods and pharaoh. Black symbolized the underworld, death, and night but it also had its positive side of replenishment and rejuvenation because of the black soil left by the annual flood. White was pure and holy, sacred and simple. In order to make these colours they used mineral compounds, oil and water, which is why they still retain their vibrant colours today. Green was made from malachite, red from oxidized iron or red ochre found in clay, blue from azurite, yellow from orpiment or yellow ochre, black from charcoal or carbon and white from gypsum or chalk.

Even though robbed out in antiquity the tombs still give an idea of the opulence and power of the rulers of this golden age. It's strange to think that in antiquity, some 2000 years ago, the tombs were a top tourist attraction even then!

The numbers given to the tombs correspond to their chronological order of discovery. Here are a few of my favourites.

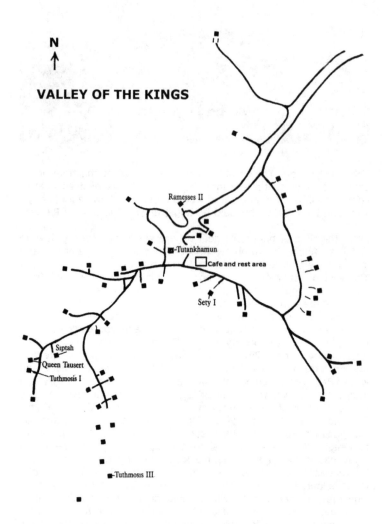

N
↑

VALLEY OF THE KINGS

Ramesses II

■-Tutankhamun

☐ Cafe and rest area

Sety I

Siptah
Queen Tausert
Tuthmosis I

■-Tuthmosis III

KV62 TUTANKHAMUN 18th Dynasty 1341-1323BC
You will have to pay extra to go into the tomb of Tutankhamun, 100LE at the time of writing. Oh yes, you have to pay more to see his lordship's tomb! To my surprise some people do actually decide

against it and I even heard one tour guide discouragingly remark to his group, 'It's really not worth the money and pretty boring as tombs go'. Personally, I think he just wanted to get away as soon as possible, as he knew there can be long queues. In my opinion, it may not be as grand, or as intriguing as some of the other tombs in the valley, but do you really want to have travelled all the way to Egypt and not see the most famous burial chamber in the Valley of the Kings?

Note: The tomb is usually closed between 1-2pm.

TIP: If you do decide to visit Tutankhamun's tomb remember to mention this to your guide when he/she is arranging a time for the group to get back together, as you will be adding an extra tomb (4 in total) to your visit and will need more time than those just doing the regular three tombs. I would try and barter for at least another 20 minutes on top of what is agreed, otherwise you will be dashing around like crazy which will completely spoil the whole experience. Because of the number of tourists, the time they give, which is usually 60 minutes is already pushing it for three tombs.

TIP: Take a printed map of the valley which shows the numbers and names of the tombs you want to visit so you can find the quickest route. (Just type 'map of valley of the kings' into Google)

Tourists making their way through the Valley of the Kings

The tomb, discovered on the 4th November 1922 by the English Egyptologist Howard Carter, is the only one in the valley not to have been robbed in antiquity. Having said that, the tomb was not found completely intact, as there appears to have been at least two robberies after the king's burial, probably carried out by some of the tomb workers.

When Lord Carnarvon, Carter's financial backer, asked if he could see anything he replied, 'Yes, I see wonderful things'.

Tutankhamun's tomb

TUTANKHAMUN BIOGRAPHY

Tutankhamun was not one of Egypt's most powerful rulers, on the contrary compared to the likes of Ramses II, he was a relatively minor king and it was only with his tomb's discovery that he became the most famous pharaoh.

As the tomb is relatively small and follows a design found more often in non-royal tombs it appears he died quite suddenly before a proper royal tomb could be prepared. Some Egyptologists believe that the tomb of King Ay, was actually the one begun for Tutankhamun but due to his sudden death they couldn't complete it in time.

Even though Tutankhamun was a relatively 'poor pharaoh' a vast fortune in treasure was still found in the tiny tomb and it makes you wonder exactly what a huge tomb like that of Ramses II must have contained!

You can tell he wasn't a particularly wealthy king because in Ancient Egypt silver was more valuable than gold and there was a relatively small amount of silver found in all of the 5000+ items recovered from the tomb.

The direct lineage of Tutankhamun is unknown. The general consensus, strongly supported by DNA evidence, is that he was the son of the heretic king Akhenaten. Whilst Tutankhamun's true family relationship remains a mystery, what there is no doubt about, is his right to the throne, as dictated by Egyptian protocol.

Originally named Tutankhaten, he was born around 1341B.C. during a time when Egypt was undergoing radical religious changes

32

brought about by Pharaoh Akhenaten who introduced monotheism, the worship of a single god named 'The Aten', in order to rid the Karnak priests of their ever-growing power and wealth. After Akhenaten's death and the early demise of his successor, Smenkhkare, Tutankhamun came to the throne at the tender age of nine.

Being so young there would have been little Tutankhamun could have done to influence events, which would have been determined by Ay, his vizier, Horemheb, his military commander, and the High Priests of Karnak. And what they did decide upon was to bring Egypt back to its traditional religion, hence the name change from Tutankhaten, meaning 'The Living Image of Aten' to Tutankhamun, 'The Living Image of Amun'.

Tutankhamun was married to Ankhesenpaaten (changed to Ankhesenamun), the third daughter of Akhenaten and Nefertiti and his possible sister.

It's believed they lived in the former palace of his grandfather Amenhotep III, on the west bank of the Nile, where the Colossi of Memnon stand. It was not their own royal residence as it would appear they spent much of their time at Memphis, his administrative centre.

A commemorative stella, (an engraved stone that was the ancient equivalent to a modern day notice-board), was set up in Karnak Temple outlining some of Tutankhamun's activities and achievements which clearly proclaimed that the priesthood had been fully re-established and the cult of Amun and other gods rightly restored to their former position. It is evident that he continued his acts of piety up until his death which included substantial projects at Karnak and Luxor temples, in particular the recording of the Opet Festival scenes on the walls of Amenhotep III's entrance colonnade.

In view of his age it's doubtful that he took part in any military campaigns, but it is thought he authorised an expedition into Palestine and Lebanon under the command of Horemheb as a show of power in order to discourage Egypt's enemies.

At the age of 18 and after only nine years of rule Tutankhamun prematurely died around 1323B.C. and with his death came the end of the royal bloodline of the eighteenth dynasty that Tutankhamun's family shared. The cause of death has never been established conclusively but many theories abound including, accident, illness, hereditary factors and assassination.

The aged Ay became his successor, followed some two to four years later by Horemheb. It is a known fact that Horemheb tried to erase the memory of Tutankhamun by the usurpation of his monuments including the stella and Opet reliefs at Karnak.

The entrance to the tomb is at the base of a sloping hill and descends via a staircase. The interior layout is a corridor and four chambers with coloured paintings and a total length is 30.79 metres. Included in the treasure were; clothing, jewellery, games,

33

furniture, alabaster sculptures, gold statues, cosmetic and perfume vessels, chariots, food, wine, hunting and warfare equipment. The coffin containing the mummy of the boy king was inside a quartzite sarcophagus and nestled within four gilded shrines. The exquisite burial mask inlaid with semi-precious stones, gold and lapis lazuli has come to symbolise the splendour and mystery of ancient Egypt. All the treasures are now held in the Museum of Antiquities at Cairo, but his body is still in situ. In fact, it is the only tomb in the Valley of the Kings that contains a mummy. You can see photographs of some of Tutankhamun's tomb treasure on our website at: www.travel-egypt.co.uk

KV34 TUTHMOSES III 18th Dynasty 1479-1425BC

Tuthmoses III tomb (KV34)

If you are in reasonable health, don't mind heights, do not suffer from claustrophobia or a bad back, then one of my favourite tombs to visit is that of Tuthmoses III. Situated quite some distance off the main track, in a narrow gorge it is certainly not an easy option, especially in the baking heat. But if you decide to give it a go you will feel as if you have achieved something. However be warned; the entrance lies some 30 metres above ground, and can only be reached via a metal staircase.

Once inside you descend down steep corridors and stairways, which involve some bending, before finally reaching the oval shaped burial chamber, reminiscent of a cartouche. The walls are decorated with scenes from the Book of Amduat that represents the twelve hours of the night and the journey Pharaoh has to undergo in order to reach the Afterlife. The Book of Amduat is the oldest amongst the tomb texts transcribed from the Valley of the Kings.

Tuthmoses III Biography:

Tuthmoses III was the sixth Pharaoh of the 18th Dynasty. However, as he was a mere child when his father died, he shared his reign with his stepmother and Aunt, Hatshepsut, for the first twenty-two years. Then, when he reached a suitable age, Hatshepsut appointed him to head the army, during which time he became a great warrior, skilled in many forms of combat and military strategy. This was a trait that would stand him in good-stead later in life, as many historians regard him as a military genius. After Hatshepsut's death he ruled Egypt alone and created the largest empire Egypt had ever seen, with no fewer than seventeen campaigns being conducted and won, from Syria in the north to Nubia in the south. Because of this, Tuthmoses III has been fondly nicknamed 'Egypt's Napoleon' by many scholars.

Many of his victories are depicted on the walls of Karnak Temple where Tuthmoses concentrated on recording his achievements. After rebuilding his grandfather's hypostyle hall (Tuthmoses I), he then went on to build two Pylons, a shrine for the bark (boat) of Amun and a jubilee hall in which to celebrate his Sed festival. He also constructed the sacred lake and commissioned several obelisks. He built his own mortuary temple near Hatshepsut's on a ledge between his stepmother's and that of Mentuhotep but it's thought a rock fall from the cliffs above may have destroyed it shortly after completion. A recent excavation of the site revealed stunningly fresh reliefs.

Up to a few years ago it was a common belief amongst historians that Tuthmoses had hated Hatshepsut with such a vengeance for keeping him from his rightful place as pharaoh, that he took great pains to deface every image he could of his stepmother in order to wipe her out of existence. However recent findings have discovered that the defilements took place some thirty years after her death making people rethink this theory, with evidence now leaning more towards the destroyer being his son, Amenhotep II. Also Hatshepsut did little to really diminish Tuthmoses' rule, as she continued to date her own rule by his regal years and continued to represent him frequently upon her monuments. Also would Hatshepsut have put the control of the army into the hands of Tuthmoses if there was such great animosity between them? Many scholars believe not.

The Sacred lake at Karnak built by Tuthmoses III

Tuthmoses' main queen was Hatshepsut-Merytre, who survived him and lived as Queen Mother into the reign of their son. Tuthmoses had five sons and at least two daughters. Officially he ruled Egypt for 54 years, from 1479 to 1425 B.C. However, this includes the first twenty two years he spent as co-regent, so alone he actually ruled for thirty two. During the final two years of his reign, he appointed his son, Amenhotep II, as co-regent. Tuthmoses would have been in his 60s when he died.

KV14 TWOSRET 19th Dynasty (Other spelling; Tausert)
Twosret's was the last Pharaoh of the 19th dynasty. Her reign was during troubled times and lasted less than three years. Twosret was the wife of Seti II and even though she was not his first wife it's believed he loved her so much that it was he who ordered her tomb to be built in the Valley of the Kings; an honour given to very few queens.
Once again succession evidence is sketchy, however the general consensus is that upon the death of her husband Queen Twosret became co-regent with the king's young son, Siptah, born to another of Seti's wives. Then some six years later around 1190 BC Siptah died and in the absence of an acceptable male heir, Twosret

ascended to the throne proclaiming herself Pharaoh. Due to her new royal status work began immediately to widen the existing tomb to the proper dimensions fit for a king, including the entrance and corridors that needed to be enlarged to accommodate the size of what was now to be a king's coffin.

Twosret's tomb entrance is located at the base of a sheer cliff in the East Valley and the interior layout is of corridors and chambers in a straight descending line to a length of 158.41 metres. Strangely the tomb is also shared with another king, Pharaoh Setnakht (reign:1185-1152BC) on the order of his son, Ramses III. Setnakht had already started work on his own tomb KV11 but when he died his son ordered his body to be interned with Twosret so he could take his father's tomb for his own. His reasoning for departing from custom is unknown, as almost all other Pharaohs buried in the Valley of the Kings built their own tombs, which they then occupied upon their deaths. So although KV14 is shared between Twosret and Setnakht the tomb was almost exclusively built for the female pharaoh.

A Royal Harem Insight:

Before becoming Pharaoh, Twosret, would have been part of the royal female *ipet*, or harem, which were private quarters devoted purely to the women of the Palace, including the first Queen, lesser wives, concubines and their children.

Presiding over all proceedings of the harem household would be the first queen, who was most likely to be of Royal birth, sometimes a half or full sister to Pharaoh. She would have also been a woman of considerable personal wealth, influence, and, as the wife of the living god on earth, highly privileged.

Surviving texts describe 'harems' as important economic organisations that were governed very much as a business. As independently governed establishments the harem formed an integral part of the palace's wealth and stability and it's therefore no great surprise to learn that on occasion it could also be a place of serious intrigue and power struggle.

One such incident involved Ramses III (1184-1153 BC) when Tiye, one of his lesser wives, planned his assassination in order to install her son onto the throne. The details of the trial have been handed down nearly complete in the 'Judicial Papyrus of Turin' which became known as the 'Harem Conspiracy'.

The papyrus contains summaries of accusations, convictions and punishments meted out. Some of the accused, amongst them Pentawer (their son) were forced to take their own lives. Another, Pebekkamen, an official serving in close proximity to the king, was executed by burning, to prevent his soul from progressing to the afterlife. Tiye's fate is not recorded but it's unlikely she was allowed to live.

37

KV11 RAMSES III   20th Dynasty 1182-1151BC

This well-preserved tomb has some of the best colours in the valley that remain remarkably vivid. It's a complex system with an unusual number of annexes. The tomb has a maximum height of 6.55m with a minimum width of 0.75m and maximum width of 13.85m. Its total length is 188.11m. The entrance has unique twin Hathor-headed columns with great twisted horns of a ram. Between them is the standard sun disc with protective goddesses, scarab and crocodile. As you enter, to your right is a chamber with boats with masts of red, blue and gold. The style is mosaic. The main ceiling after the first ramp is in very good condition with cartouches down the centre and lines of gods on either side. The second chamber on the right depicts a storage area with jars for wine and beer. The third has a kingfisher on a boat and the fourth images of Osiris and Isis. The four pillared hall is decorated with scenes from the Book of Gates and various large deities. The final corridor is inscribed with material from the 'Opening of the Mouth' ceremony and the burial chamber has decorations from the Book of Gates and the Book of the Earth. The above mentioned 'books' were all funerary texts describing how the deceased entered the afterlife. On the way out there is a depiction of a three-headed serpent. In one side chamber there is a representation of a perfumery with lotus flowers, fruits and weighing scales. In another there are musical instruments with cobras and a bull. The tomb is often referred to as the 'Tomb of the Harpists' due to the bas-relief of two blind musicians located in one of the side chambers.

HISTORY OF ANCIENT EGYPTAIN MUSICAL INSTRUMENTS

Music played a very important part in this highly developed social and cultural country. In Egypt instruments were usually identified with the primary deities such as Hathor, Isis and Sekhmet and these deities would often be shown playing musical instruments such as the sistrum, drum and menit. Whether out in the street, in the temple, the palace or tombs, music was used in all religious, celebratory and entertainment venues.

Rhythmic music was used in most religious practices such as liturgy, rituals and processions. Pictorial evidence would suggest that many musicians were women. During the New Kingdom these females were highly trained and employed by large temples as priestesses and were known by the name 'sem'ayt'. Usually they were the wives or daughters of the priests and held titles such as, 'Song-stress of Amun' and became quite powerful in their own right, holding high positions close to Pharaoh with the highest musician bearing the title 'Chief of the Singers of Pharaoh'. Male musicians were often shown in a more military context, such as drummers or trumpeters. All of the temple hierarchy were devoted to solemn hymns and prayers, most of which were accompanied by music and often performed to create a spell (a heka), or afford protection. The two main gods of 'music and dancing' were the female goddess Hathor and Bes (male). All music was called 'Hy' which meant joy or gladness, whilst the name for sound was "herw", meaning voice.

The most common instruments in use were;

- The sistrum (or sistra), predominantly a female instrument, is thought to have evolved from the archaic ritual of cutting papyrus stems and rattling them together rhythmically to 'open one's heart to Hathor'. Held in the hand they were shaken to make a sound not unlike that of a tambourine. The word sistrum means to sway to and fro, to vibrate. Made of wood, metal or ceramic it had a handle and a top half where bands of metal were fixed so they jingled when the instrument was shaken. Sistrums were particularly used in rituals relating to the Egyptian gods and goddesses and were often accompanied by chanting. The sistrum was the main instrument employed by the Egyptian priestess.

Sistrums came in various shapes and sizes

- Cymbals, not dissimilar to our modern version in design, were usually used in combination with drums and sistrums and would have sounded more like small hand bells. Unlike the vast majority of non-tuned modern cymbals, ancient ones were tuned to a specific musical note. Neither were they struck full against each other, but by one of their edges. Different sized cymbals would produce different notes and sound effects.
- Clappers were made of wood or ivory and used widely in military, spiritual and religious events. They were the equivalent of the modern castanet. In depictions from the Old Kingdom grapes are shown being trod to the rhythm provided by clappers. Clappers were later used in dances, and festivals to keep time. Very often clappers would be carved from a single hippopotamus tusk sawn down the middle. Specimens of such percussion instruments have been recorded from prehistoric times onward. Included among the treasures buried with Tutankhamun was a pair of ivory clappers found on the floor of the Annex, and inscribed with the names of Queen Tiye and Merytaten thought to be his grandmother and sister. These instruments were typically carved in the form of a pair of gently curving human hands and forearms. A hole in each of the upper forearms allows for a cord to hold the two

clappers together and the noise would have been produced by shaking. Images from 4000 **BC** would indicate that the curved-blade clappers were held in one hand, with the average length being around 7 inches.

Tutankhamun's Ivory clappers

- The Menit was a ceremonial object associated with the goddess Hathor. The temple priestesses would be shown holding the 'Menit necklace', which comprised of a number of strands of beads gathered into a counterpoint. It's believed that the menit was used as a kind of percussion instrument in certain ceremonies and accompanied the dances that were performed to heal, restore equilibrium and please the senses. The sound would have been not unlike that of a rattle. Discovered in the tomb of Tutankhamun, we see a scene where his wife is holding a sistrum and menit before Pharaoh. Also during the festival of Hathor the priestesses would go from door to door shaking the instrument in order to bring long life, health, and rebirth to the occupants.
- Barrel-shaped drums were the domain of military musicians who were highly skilled. As yet, no representations of drums being played with sticks have been found. The round frame drum first appears in Egypt around 1400BC and some have survived. Quite often they would be painted with symbolic scenes, which illustrated the drum's influence on evoking resurrection, creation and the natural rhythms of the universe. The beat of the drum was used to coordinate the rhythms of oarsmen on the boats that sailed the Nile. Also in ritual processions priestesses are often depicted playing the frame drum as they accompanied the sacred boats of the deities. A stone relief from the Ptolemaic period show priestesses playing the frame drum before Isis, whilst another depicts four women giving praise to the goddesses Hathor and Mut. The frame drum would have been played in all of the main temples such as; Dendera, Karnak, Edfu and Philae. Many have been found in tombs amongst the deceased's burial goods.
- The harp, one of the oldest musical instruments, can be seen depicted on wall paintings in Ancient Egyptian tombs that date back to 3000 BC. They are thought to have been developed from the ancient hunting bow.

40

Female musicians with harp, lute flute and lyre (Not a scene from KV11)

- The flute, probably invented by an Egyptian, was amongst the first musical instruments used by the ancients and was made of Nile bamboo. Some ancient Egyptian flutes have survived, preserved in tombs. Like modern flutes, the Egyptians blew the instrument through an opening at one end and produced the notes by means of 5 to 7 side holes. Double flutes made of two unequal sized parallel pipes had been known since the Old Kingdom, with the longer pipe producing different pitched notes than the shorter one. Some flutes were very long, with the performer generally sitting on the ground in order to play them.
- The lute has strings stretched along a neck attached to a resonating body. Again they have been found in Egyptian art, appearing in the archaeological New Kingdom period of the 18th Dynasty (1540-1307 BC). It is generally believed that the lute may have been introduced into Egypt. Classed as long necked lutes, the ancient Egyptian instruments generally had 2/3 strings (probably made of thin leather), a long stick neck and a drum-like body covered with animal skin. The neck was round, with or without frets. A small handful have survived.
- The first metal trumpets are attributed to the Egyptians, The ancient name for the trumpet was, 'sheneb'. Eighteenth Dynasty artists drew them in tombs as short straight instruments made of wood or metal. These types of trumpets were mainly used for military signalling such as to direct and manage troops, encourage engagement and intimidate the enemy. Egyptian trumpeters are often shown in pairs and were the domain of men. The oldest surviving examples of metallic trumpets are the two instruments that were excavated during

Tutankhamun's silver trumpet

the discovery of the tomb of Tutankhamun in 1922 by Howard Carter. One, made of silver, was found wrapped in a reed cover and left in the southeast corner of the burial chamber outside the outermost golden shrine, it measures 58.2cms long, whilst the other, made of copper is 50.5 cm and was found in a long chest in the Antechamber. Both have wooden stoppers inserted within the bell end, probably to help protect the shape when not being played. Both are also inscribed with the most powerful Egyptian gods, Ra-Harakhty, Amun-Ra, Ptah and the King himself. The mouthpieces are a cylindrical sleeve with a ring at the outer end and fixed to the outside of the tube; they are not cup-shaped or detachable. Vibrating the lips onto the fixed amplifying mouthpiece would have created the sound, which has been described as raucous and powerful, rhythmic and of single pitch. In 1939 famous recordings were made of both the silver and copper trumpets by the BBC played by a military bandsman, James Tappern of the 11th Prince Albert's own Hussars. Unfortunately the use of a modern mouthpiece that was inserted into the silver trumpet and the force required to play shattered the three thousand year old instrument. Fortunately the trumpet was repaired to such a high standard by the firm Lucas that it would be played again in the Cairo Museum by another renowned trumpeter, Philip Jones. He reported that the sound was not melodious as the bore in relationship to the length of the trumpet was not proportional, but that it was probably the most thrilling experience he had ever had as a trumpet player. The trumpets have no valves and the lowest notes that could be clearly sounded were D and C respectively. It was common for instruments in antiquity to be of a single pitch and it had only been the use of the modern mouthpiece by James Tappern that had enabled a wider range of notes. A third trumpet thought to date from the Ptolemaic period, is held in the Louvre Museum in Paris, France. You can find a downloadable recording of the 1939 BBC trumpet playing on our website.

You can also take advantage of an exclusive offer on our original Egyptian music CD – 'Eternal River' which is currently only available from our websites.

ETERNAL RIVER by STEVEN WOOD
Music to Sail the Nile By

Save on the Normal RRP of £8.99

Special Discount Only Available Through This Book

To take advantage of this special offer use the link below

www.travel-egypt.co.uk/cd-offer.php

If you are looking for something special to listen to during your Egyptian holiday then I would suggest our 'Eternal River' music which is available for download from our website. The music is ideal for use with any mp3 player, iPod or to burn to your own CD. This Ancient Egyptian inspired music has been especially written for us and is presently only available from our websites, where you can listen to samples.

VALLEY OF THE QUEENS

Next on the agenda could be the Valley of the Queens, where again three tombs are usually included. It should be noted that on my last visit there were only three tombs open! Personally, I find the Valley of the Queens not particularly interesting and its title a little misleading as the vast majority of the people buried there are nobles or princes and princesses, not queens. In ancient times, it was known as Ta-Set-Neferu, meaning, the place of the Children of the Pharaoh'.

The tombs of these individuals were maintained by mortuary priests who performed daily rituals and provided offerings and prayers for the deceased nobility. This necropolis holds more than seventy tombs from the 18th, 19th and 20th Dynasties, many of which are stylishly decorated with deities and hieroglyphs. The hieroglyphs language consists of some 20 letters and over 700 pictorial representations.

It should be noted that the famous and lavishly decorated Nefertari tomb, QV66, will not be included in your tour as the burial chamber is no longer open to the public and requires special permission from the SCA (Supreme Council of Antiquities) to unlock it.

In 2003 the tomb closed completely to visitors for an indefinite period in order to investigate the condition of the painted walls which were deteriorating due to mould growing on their surface. It's believed the fungus was being caused by bacteria in visitors' breath and settling on the wall's surface.

Nefertari was one of the principle wives of Ramses II whom he married before ascending to the throne. They had at least four sons and two daughters together. Her name means 'Beautiful Companion'.

Along with Cleopatra, Nefertiti and Hatshepsut she is one of the best known Egyptian queens.

MORTUARY TEMPLE OF HATSHEPSUT (DEIR EL BAHRI)

The mortuary temples of the New Kingdom pharaohs were all built at the edge of the desert at Thebes. Unfortunately a great number have perished but a few still remain and are a true testament to the splendour that once was Egypt. One such temple is that of the female Pharaoh Hatshepsut and I have no doubt that at some stage during your visit you will be driven a short distance to the antiquity site. Here visitors make their way up a long tarmac road to reach this magnificent temple whilst trying to side step as many of the local tradesman as possible who are there everyday peddling their wares. Temperatures at the temple can be very high with little chance of shade so take plenty of bottled water, sun cream and a hat. If you prefer there are motorised carriages that ferry people to and from the temple rather than you having to walk in the sweltering heat.

The Mortuary temple took fifteen years to construct and Hatshepsut chose her chancellor, Senenmut, as chief architect and engineer. Of low birth Senenmut's importance at the royal court under Hatshepsut is surprising and unquestionable and many believe he was her lover, given the privileges granted to him under her reign.

The stunning Mortuary Temple consists of three colonnaded terraces of perfect harmony that were once graced with superb gardens. Sited within a magnificent natural amphitheatre and built directly into a cliff face the complex is considered to be one of the greatest buildings of the ancient world.

The temple's uppermost tier has now been reopened to the public after many years of closure due to excavation and restoration. As you look at the temple you will note at ground level the two sides are slightly different in colour, with the left-hand side being somewhat redder. This was caused by recent poor restoration work being carried out by a Polish team. When I last visited there was still some restoration work in progress but it didn't interfere with people's enjoyment. Remember to take your camera and camcorder as both are presently allowed at the temple.

The long hot walk to the Temple of Hatshepsut

TEMPLE OF HATSHEPSUT
Deir el Bahri

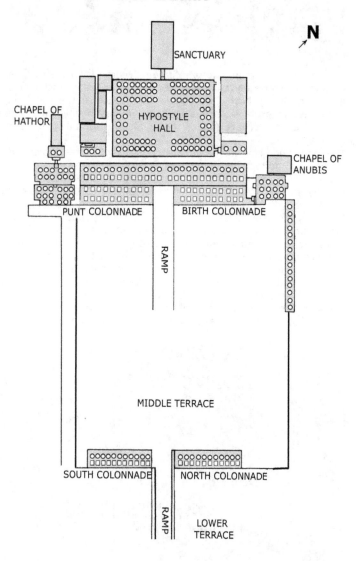

N

SANCTUARY

CHAPEL OF HATHOR

HYPOSTYLE HALL

CHAPEL OF ANUBIS

PUNT COLONNADE

BIRTH COLONNADE

RAMP

MIDDLE TERRACE

SOUTH COLONNADE

NORTH COLONNADE

RAMP

LOWER TERRACE

HATSHEPSUT'S BIOGRAPHY:

Being a royal woman in Ancient Egypt did not exclude you from the throne, unlike the vast majority of kingdoms at that time. Ancient Egyptian women had great advantages over their contemporaries in other cultures, such as Mesopotamia and Greece as they were able to own property, inherit wealth, defend their legal rights in court and hold official positions. As the famous Greek Herodotus pointed out much to his horror, 'Egyptian women were free to move about in public unlike her Greek counterpart who were confined to the home'. However, it is generally regarded that if a woman did become pharaoh it was because she probably had the backing of some very influential men.

Hatshepsut was one of the most important female pharaohs of Egypt. She ruled during the early part of the 18th Dynasty, an exciting time known as the 'Golden Age of Egypt' that includes many of the best known pharaohs and queens, including King Tutankhamun, Amenhotep, Tiye, Akhenaton and Nefertiti.

Hatshepsut was the daughter of Tuthmoses I and Queen Ahmose. Upon the death of her father, who is believed to have died from an arrowhead lodged in his chest, his son Tuthmoses II succeeded him and as was the custom, he married his stepsister, Hatshepsut, in order to preserve the royal blood line. They had no sons, only a daughter. When Tuthmoses II also died, from an alleged wound to the neck and chronic heart disease, his son Tuthmoses III, by another wife, became Pharaoh. However as the new pharaoh was a minor, Hatshepsut stepped in as his guardian and a co-regency was formed. This lasted approximately a year before Hatshepsut took full control and appointed herself Pharaoh.

In order to legitimise her role she used a number of strategies, including having herself depicted as a man wearing the traditional regalia of the pharaohs, including false beard, the crown of two lands and kilt. She also claimed that the god Amun had visited her mother whilst pregnant proclaiming that it was the will of the god that Hatshepsut be Pharaoh, which effectively made her a divine child.

During her very successful fifteen-year reign Hatshepsut's trade expeditions were ground breaking and her building work was on a scale that had never been seen before. She initiated a number of impressive projects, including her superb funerary temple at Deir el-Bahri and several structures at Karnak and Luxor Temples. In fact, it's quite possible that she was the founder of the latter. Yet another remarkable achievement was the transportation of two huge granite obelisks on the River Nile from Aswan to the Temple of Karnak.

During her sovereignty Hatshepsut mounted at least one military campaign but perhaps her greatest achievement was the expedition that she orchestrated to the Land of Punt, which is recorded on the walls of her mortuary temple. Amongst other priced possessions it shows ebony, ivory, myrrh saplings, animal

47

skins, incense, gold, perfumes and exotic animals being brought back from a land believed to have been located near the Red Sea and present-day Somalia.

Lion on the walls of Hatshepsut's temple

Hatshepsut holding the royal flail and crook, emblems of the god Osiris and symbols of divine authority. The goddess Hathor worshipped at Deir el-Bahri

Unlike the warlike temperament of many of her 18th dynasty counterparts Hatshepsut devoted herself to administration, the encouragement of commerce and trade and will be forever

48

immortalised by the illustrations at Deir el Bahri that are said to be so exquisitely detailed that even fish species can be identified from the drawings.

Even though Hatshepsut was a powerful and admirable woman who increased her country's wealth and brought great stability to Egypt she mysteriously disappears around 1458 BC, when Tuthmoses III regained his title as Pharaoh. Because someone ordered all reference to Hatshepsut be wiped from Egyptian history her images were defiled, her statues smashed and her mummy removed from its tomb, which meant her name was nearly lost to the annals of history forever. Although her grandfather, father, husband and stepson mummies have all been found, Hatshepsut's mummy has never been positively identified and remains one of Egypt's many mysteries yet to be resolved.

Hatshepsut Mummy Claim:

Hatshepsut's tomb (KV20) was documented by Belzoni but it was the English archaeologist Howard Carter who first excavated it whilst working at the Valley of the Kings in 1902. However it wasn't until 1920 that he properly explored its interior, which resulted in the discovery of two sarcophagi, one for Hatshepsut and the second for her father, both of which were empty. The tomb, some 35 storeys underground, is the deepest in Egypt and probably the world.

Although a badly worn mural you can still see the outline of a boat and oarsmen. Hatshepsut sent a fleet of five ships to Punt, each with thirty rowers.

In 1903 Carter had also found and opened a separate tomb now known as KV60, where he found coffins of mummified geese and the partially disturbed and decaying coffins of two women lying side by side. One bore the inscription of Sitre-In, Hatshepsut's wet nurse, the other was anonymous. As the tomb was not deemed to be Royal it received little attention until Egyptologist Donald Ryan reopened it in 1989. The sarcophagus marked with the name of the

49

wet nurse was taken to Cairo museum, and the second unnamed sarcophagus remained behind.

In 2007 the tomb was reopened for Discovery Television and the remaining sarcophagus was removed and taken to Cairo for a CT scan. The scan revealed that this mummy was an obese woman aged between 45 and 60, who had suffered with bad teeth and diabetes. It was determined that she had died from cancer, evidence of which could be seen in the pelvic region and spine, indicating that it had spread throughout her body. The scanner was also used to examine artefacts including a small wooden box that bore the cartouche of Hatshepsut and contained a liver and tooth. An Egyptian dentist studied the scans of the tooth and noted that the fat lady from KV60 was also missing a tooth and that the hole left behind and the type of tooth that was missing was a match for the loose one in the box. Speculation was also fuelled by the fact the mummy's left arm was bent in a pose thought to mark royal burials. Upon this evidence Mr Hawass declared that the mummy in KV60 was that of Hatshepsut.

However many renowned archaeologists have expressed scepticism. It should be noted that at the time of completing the documentary the DNA evidence had not been conclusive and further DNA investigation has still not been made known (2011), nor published in any reputable peer-reviewed scientific journal — the gold standard of scientific research worldwide.

So, until there is conclusive DNA evidence, the jury is still out as to whether Hatshepsut's mummy has been found - even though your Egyptian tour guide may insist differently! And the mummy has been added to the royal mummies at the Cairo Museum.

Other possible venues during your visit to the Theban Necropolis could be;

MORTUARY TEMPLE OF RAMSES III (MEDINET HABU)

This mortuary temple is one of my favourite ancient sites at Thebes. The ancient Egyptian name for the area was Djanet (meaning Men and mothers) and it was said to be the place where Amun appeared for the first time.

Both Hatshepsut and Tuthmoses III built small temples dedicated to Amun, probably on the ruins of a much older temple, and later Ramses III built his large mortuary temple.

Medinet Habu is the best preserved of all mortuary temples in the Necropolis and was called 'The Mansion of Millions of Years'.

It is a magnificent complex containing two courtyards, Hypostyle Hall, sanctuaries, Palace ruins, small chapels, nilometer, sacred lake, storehouses, workshops, administrative offices, residences of priests and officials all enclosed by large mud brick walls. The temple measures approximately 700 by 1000 feet and was entered by two gates on the east and west sides of the mud brick enclosure. The eastern entrance was fronted by a quayside which allowed boats to dock and load or unload cargo and passengers via the canals that were fed from the Nile.

Smaller chapel (left) built by the Hatshepsut with Ramses III's huge mortuary temple in the background and sacred lake in foreground

Djanet was also believed to be the holy site where the first primeval gods, known as the Ogdoad, were buried. On the 'Feast of the Tenth Day', rituals performed at Djanet by priests gave the Ogdoad new life and thereby renewed creation. (See our 'Egyptian Mythology' section)

MORTUARY TEMPLE OF SETI I (c 1294-1279 BC)
The memorial temple of Seti I seems to have been constructed towards the end of the reign on Seti, and may have been completed by his son Ramses the Great (II) after his father's death.
To the southern part of the temple one of the chambers contained a shrine/sanctuary dedicated to Seti's father Ramses I, who ruled for less than two years and who didn't construct a mortuary temple for himself.
It should be remembered that the implementation of funerary art in mortuary temples varies little as it was inherited from long-established traditions and was considered sacred, therefore similar themes follow on from one dynasty to the next with the only real difference lying in the competence and complexity of its deliverance.
The temple was built of sandstone on the traditional plan of two courtyards, each with their own pylon, a six columned hypostyle hall and a sanctuary which has four simple square pillars and decoration depicting Seti offering incense before the boat of Amun. Originally the temple would have been approached by an avenue of sphinxes but only one now remains, which is inscribed with a motif of nine bows, representing Seti's conquered enemies. Near the

entrance there are several stele (basically stone 'notice boards'), bearing carvings and inscriptions about Seti I, Ramses I and II. The entire court and any pylons associated with it have long since been destroyed.

Much of Seti's mortuary temple is in ruins

SETI I BIOGRAPHY

Pharaoh Seti I was the son of Ramses I and Queen Sitre. The name Seti means 'of Set', indicating his connection with the god Seth. In battle he fought with great determination and generally concluded his military campaigns victoriously.

During his lifetime he confronted the Libyans, Syrians, Nubians and Hittites in an effort to win back the empire of Tuthmoses III and succeeded in retaking many lost and disputed territories from as far afield as Mesopotamia to Cyprus, bringing home vast treasures to adorn his temple and palaces.

Seti I was considered a great king, but his fame and achievements has been somewhat overshadowed by that of his son, Ramses II. The traditional view of Seti I's reign is that he restored the Egyptian Empire to a time before it was lost during the rule of the monotheistic king, Akhenaton.

Seti's tomb, discovered by Giovanni Battista Belzoni on 16 October 1817 in the Valley of the Kings (KV17), is one of the best decorated but is usually closed to the public due to damage caused first by Jean-François Champollion, (translator of the Rosetta Stone), who physically removed two large wall sections during his 1828-29 expedition and then by excavations in the late 1950s early

60s that caused walls to crack or collapse as the work created significant changes in the moisture levels within the tomb. The tomb is often referred to as the 'Apis Tomb' because a mummified bull was found in a side room off the main burial hall. Seti's extremely well preserved mummy lies in state at the Museum of Antiquities, Cairo and it appears he was less than forty years old when he died. The cause of his death is unknown but it has been suggested that he died from a disease which possibly affected his heart, which was found in the right side of the body, as opposed to the left side where it was normal placed by the embalmers during the mummification process. Seti's mummy is about 5 ft 7 inches tall.

MORTUARY TEMPLE OF RAMSES II (RAMESSEUM) Reign 1279 to 1213 BC

This mortuary temple was built by Ramses II and has become known as the Ramesseum. Architecturally, the design of the mortuary temple adheres to the standard rule of the New Kingdom. Oriented northwest and southeast, the temple itself comprises of two stone gateways, one after the other, each leading into its own courtyard. Beyond the second courtyard, at the centre of the complex, is a 48-column covered hypostyle hall (only 39 remain), which surrounds the inner sanctuary. Only part of the first room, containing a ceiling decorated with astral scenes, remains, with the second and third in ruins. As was custom, the temple is decorated with scenes commemorating pharaoh's military victories, in particular the Battle of Kadesh (ca.1285 BC), plus his dedication and kinship to the gods, which effectively proclaimed his own immortality.

Fallen statue at the Ramesseum

In earlier times it was said that three great monolithic statues fronted the temple and in particular the seated statue of the king himself surpassed, in size, all other statues in Egypt.

53

Diodorus, a Greek historian who lived in the 1st century BC, wrote the *Bibliotheca Historica* a history of the world in 40 books and in volume one he describes the history and culture of Ancient Egypt. Of the largest Ramesseum statue he remarked, 'The work was wonderful, not only for its size but for the art and also the excellence of the stone in which, huge though it was, there was neither crack nor blemish'. Sadly the statue has long since collapsed and the upper part fallen into ruin.

Diodorus also tells of a library that was attached to the temple that he refers to as 'The Medicine of the Mind', which was located at the back of the temple and formed part of a large number of external buildings which included temple palace, chapels, storerooms, granaries, workshops, and other ancillary buildings. There is also evidence that indicates the temple was the site of an important school for scribes. Traditionally the entire complex was enclosed in mud brick walls.

The site was in use before Ramses II as archaeologist Flinders Petrie found a shaft tomb in 1895 that dated from the Middle Kingdom and yielded a rich hoard of religious and funerary artifacts, including the Ramesseum papyri which have been described as the 'most precious single find of papyri' from pharaonic Egypt.

The papyrus texts, some 136 items, comprise the archive of the tomb-owner who was probably a priest. The writings span a wide range of topics, many of which alluded to ceremonial and healing text that may have reflected the priest's professional activities as ritual equipment were also found with the papyri.

Amongst the scrolls was also found the papyrus of 'The Tale of Sinuhe', which is considered to be one of the finest works of Ancient Egyptian literature. Set in the aftermath of the death of Pharaoh Amenemhat I, founder of the 12th dynasty (1937-1908 BC), the general consensus is that it is most likely a work of fiction although there is an ongoing debate among Egyptologists as to whether or not the tale is based on actual events.

Either way the tale is considered to be a work written in verse, whose ideas have many parallels in biblical texts and may also have been performed, which has had the anonymous author likened to Shakespeare.

The great popularity of the work is witnessed by the numerous surviving fragments which are mostly held in the British Museum.

RAMSES II BIOGRAPHY:

Ramses II is often regarded as Egypt's greatest, most celebrated and powerful pharaoh, even his successors referred to him as the 'Great Ancestor'.

It's believed he ascended the throne in his early 20s and is known to have ruled Egypt for a total of 66 years and lived into his 90s. It's also known that he celebrated at least fourteen Sed Festivals during his reign, an unprecedented number and more than any other pharaoh. The Sed (or Heb-Sed) festival was an ancient Egyptian ceremony which was held to celebrate the continued rule of a pharaoh after he had been on the throne for thirty years and then every three years after.

Ramses II embarked on numerous campaigns against the Syrians, Libyans, Nubians, Shardana Sea Pirates, Palestinians and Hittites in order to secure Egypt's borders. During his reign, the Egyptian army is estimated to have totaled about 100,000 men, a formidable force.

Ramses II built great monuments across the Egyptian empire, most notably Abu Simbel and the Ramesseum. Under his reign his country was more prosperous and powerful than it had been in nearly a century. The most important and famous of his royal wives was Nefertari, to whom he dedicated a temple at Abu Simbel. When he died he was buried in the Valley of the Kings but his mummy is now on display in the Cairo Museum. His tomb has been proven to be the largest in the Valley of the Kings and originally contained the remains of some of this king's estimated 52 sons. It's thought he sired over 100 children during his lifetime.

WORKERS VILLAGE (DEIR EL MEDINA) A NONE ROYAL SITE

The workers village is a fascinating place to visit. The fact it's the remains of buildings used by the common people, rather than royals, makes it an archaeological gem. Here you can walk up the main street that runs through the centre of this amazing array of houses that were inhabited by the people who worked daily in the Valley of the Kings, giving you an unparalleled impression of what life was like for the people who excavated, built and decorated the tombs.

Remains of the village

55

In 1922 a team led by Bernard Bruyère began to excavate the site, which resulted in one of the most thoroughly documented accounts of life in the ancient world, detailing both social interactions and the working and living conditions of a community.

The settlement's ancient name was *St-maat-hr-imenty-Waset* (The Place of Truth to the West of Thebes) and the workmen who lived there were called, 'Servants in the Place of Truth'. These artisans were highly skilled craftsman who passed down the knowledge of their trade from father to son through many generations, beginning as far back as the reign of Tuthmoses I. Sculptors, stone masons, draughtsmen, painters, plasterers, all would have lived in the village.

Tomb inscriptions, stella, papyri, and ostraca (inscribed pottery, equivalent to modern day notepaper) were found in the village and surrounding area, all serving to give a picture of what life was like for the villagers. There were also many small shrines and chapels discovered dedicated to various deities, including Ptah, Bes and Het-Hert, attesting to the devotion of the families living there.

The village was laid out in a square grid within mud-brick walls and is believed to have been isolated from the general population because, as builders of the royal tombs, they were considered to hold the key to many sensitive secrets, such as insider knowledge of tomb locations and contents.

Together with their wives and families the workmen occupied the 70 or so neatly constructed houses of mud brick and stone for some 450 years during Egypt's affluent New Kingdom period.

FURTHER VISITS

You will not be able to see all of the ancient sites the Necropolis has to offer during your visit and what you do see will be governed by various factors such as; company policy, guide, allotted time, popularity and closures. What I would therefore suggest is if you have any spare time, say towards the end of your holiday, then use it to make a return visit to the West Bank. You can easily hire a private taxi to take you to the places you missed on the first visit but ensure you agree a round trip price with the taxi driver before leaving and stipulate that you want him to wait whilst you visit the sites. Also, make sure he is agreeing to a fee in Egyptian pounds, not English!! Alternatively, your holiday rep will be able to book a taxi for you at an agreed price. It may cost you a little more, but it will cut out the hassle of having to haggle, especially if you are not comfortable with it. I would also strongly recommend that you acquaint yourself with the West Bank sites before you visit, so you know exactly what you want to see. You will find a list of recommended travel guidebooks on our website.

An average time for a visit to the West Bank is four-five hours and on arrival back at the boat lunch will be served, after which the rest of the afternoon is usually spent leisurely, as you recuperate after your early morning start. However if you are still in an explorative mood you could always take a trip into town. I tend to utilise the spare time checking out hotels and amenities for future reference.

Stone stella - the Ancient's equivalent of a modern day notice board

DAY TWO:

TEMPLES DEDICATED TO THE GODS (EAST BANK)
Whilst you are still moored up at Luxor your tour guide will arrange a combined trip to the two main temples in the vicinity, namely Karnak and Luxor. As opposed to the mortuary temple on the west bank which we have just discussed, the religious temples on the east bank of Thebes were dedicated to the gods, not pharaoh.
As a point of interest Thebes, modern day Luxor, was the name the Greeks gave to the town. The historian Homer described it as, 'The City of the Hundred Gates'. The Ancient Egyptian name for the city was 'Waset'.
You trip will start around 8am, after an early breakfast and last approximately four hours. Be sure to take your camera/camcorder as there are no restrictions on photography in either temple.

PRECINCT OF AMUN:
MAIN TOURIST AREA OF KARNAK TEMPLE

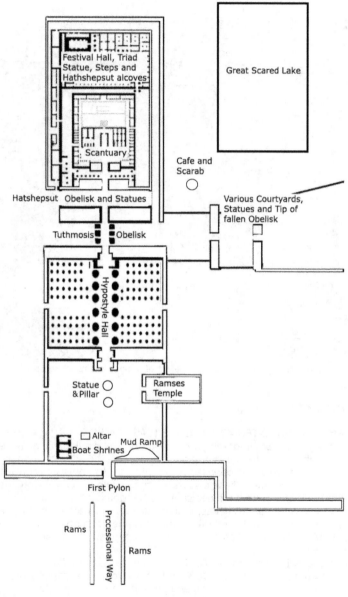

KARNAK TEMPLE

By far the larger of the two temples is Karnak, which was built and added to by approximately thirty rulers, including Hatshepsut, Tuthmoses III and Ramses II. The temples construction, carried out over a fourteen hundred year period, beginning with the Middle Kingdom and ending with the Ptolemaic era, which enabled it to reach a size, complexity, and diversity unparalleled in the world.

In ancient times the temple was called, *Ipet-Isut* (The Most Select of Places) and was dedicated to the ancient deity, Amun.

Best explained as a series of temples its total ground cover is approximately 247 acres and in its heyday it would have boasted thousands of staff, including priests, servants, dancers, gardeners, craftsmen etc. Although badly ruined, this huge religious complex is my favourite ancient Egyptian site, an incredibly imposing and wonderful place that I never tire of.

As a centre of worship the temple was governed by priests who carried out a series of daily rituals to honour the god Amun, along with performing annual festivals and celebrations. The daily rituals would involve cleansing, presentations, chanting, offerings, prayer, purifications, burning of incense, and the pouring of libation. All enacted in order to satisfy and placate the deity and ensure continued favour and protection.

Ram Road – the entrance to the Precinct of Amun Ra and Karnak Temple

Although the common belief is that Pharaoh was rarely around for these daily ceremonies he was the link between the divine realm and humanity and therefore it is he who is shown executing the offerings on the walls of Karnak.

59

A shrine and golden god statue. The god would be sealed into the large shrine within the main sanctuary.

In ancient time, during the Opet festival, Amun's statue would be carried on a barge by priests from Karnak to Luxor Temple, where the god would be 'reunited' with his goddess wife, Mut. In Ancient Egypt every religious temple would have a triad of gods associated with it. At Karnak these were Amun, King of the Gods, Mut, goddess of retribution, and their son Khonsu, god of the moon and time.

In front of the first pylon (large outer wall) is a row of rams, which represent the god Amun. Passing through the first pylon you enter an open courtyard. This was as far as any commoner could go and even this was only allowed on special occasions. To the left is a small chapel built by Seti II as a resting-place for the boats of the Theban Triad that were carried around during festivals. It has three entrances, one for each bark (boat). The doorway in the middle opens onto a long narrow chamber and as the largest of the three it would have housed the boat of Amun. In front of the chapel is a sacrificial altar that was used for animals. Against the right pylon wall you will see a large mound of harden mud that clearly demonstrates how the ancients built and decorated the huge walls by using the mud as a ramp. The large central stone column is the only remaining pillar that formed part of a structure built during the reign of Taharqa of the 25th Dynasty. The large statue is Ramses II and to the right is his temple. The avenue of ram-headed sphinxes continues on from the outside into the courtyard.

Hypostyle Hall and Sacrificial Altar. Egyptians never used human sacrifice

The 'cult statue' of Amun to whom all the daily rituals were preformed, was housed within the innermost sanctuary of the temple and was believed to contain that god's ka, or 'life force'. Some of the known festivals celebrated at Karnak were; 'The Festival of Amun', 'New Year Festival', 'First and Sixth Day Festivals', 'Festival of Mut' and 'Opet Festival'.

Reached through the Second Pylon, the Great Hypostyle Hall is considered to be one of the world's greatest architectural masterpieces, with its 134 massive columns arranged in 16 rows. In ancient times a ceiling covered the hall, which would have made it a very dark and mysterious place. The inner reliefs throughout the hall contain images of worship and offerings, whilst the outer walls are covered with victorious battle and hunting scenes.

Construction began during the reign of Ramses I, with the work being continued by his son, Seti I, and then completed by his son, Ramses II. However, as the twelve central columns are taller than the rest, some researchers believe that Amenhotep III was the initial builder and later pharaohs just added to the site.

Karnak has the largest sacred lake in Egypt and it was here that Pharaoh's ritual boat would be ceremoniously rowed. In ancient times the lake would have had its own royal flock of geese.

Unfortunately not all the areas of the temple are open to the public, just the Precinct of Amun Ra, which is often mistakenly referred to as Karnak Temple, because this is the only part most visitors normally see.

61

The three other parts, the Precinct of Mut, the Precinct of Montu, and the dismantled Temple of Amenhotep IV are all closed to the public.

Sacred Lake

In ancient times avenues of sphinx connected the Precinct of Amun to the Precinct of Mut, and onwards to Luxor Temple.

The ruined sphinx avenue that once ran all the way from Karnak to Luxor Temple. (Now closed to the public) The avenue is under restoration.

LUXOR TEMPLE
Located in the centre of the town, approximately a mile from Karnak, is Luxor Temple. This temple is a much smaller and intimate site that runs parallel to the river.
In ancient Egypt it was known by the name *Ipet-Resut* which translates into; 'The Southern Sanctuary'.

Outside the temple there is an avenue of sphinx that at one time would have linked up with the ones in the photo above at Karnak.

Sphinx lined road outside Luxor Temple built by Nectanebo I

Courtyard of Ramses II

The earliest part of the temple still standing are the boat chapels behind the first pylon which were built by Hatshepsut and Tuthmoses III (18th Dynasty). The central part of the site, which includes the colonnade and sun court, was built by Amenhotep III (18th Dynasty). During the 19th Dynasty Ramses II added the entrance pylon and two obelisks, one of which now resides in France. To the rear of the temple are chapels built by Tuthmoses III and Alexander. During the later Roman era, the temple and its surroundings became a fortress and centre of government.

The very impressive inner courtyard with statues of Pharaoh and the gods

Sphinx Avenue and main entrance to Luxor temple

Courtyard of Amenhotep III

LUXOR TEMPLE

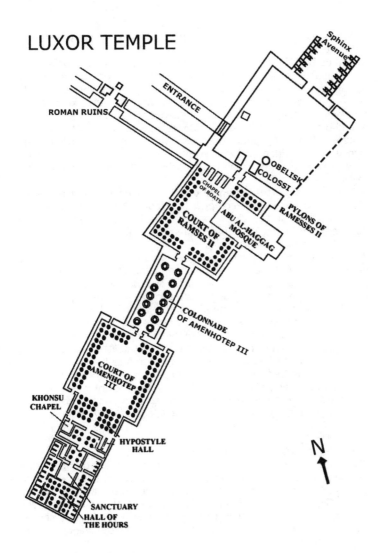

AMENHOTEP III BIOGRAPHY

As the ninth pharaoh from the 18th Dynasty who ruled between 1380 -1349 B.C. Amenhotep appears to have been crowned whilst still a child, probably around the age of 12. His first wife was Tiy, the daughter of a provincial official, whom he married two years into his reign. Throughout his reign Queen Tiy featured prominently alongside the king. It's believed they had two sons and at least four daughters, maybe five. He was the son of Tuthmoses IV, the father of Amenhotep IV (Akhenaten) and possibly grandfather or father to Tutankhamun.

Amenhotep III's reign was a period of unprecedented prosperity and artistic splendour, when Egypt reached the peak of her artistic and international power. His reign passed by relatively peacefully with the only recorded military activity by the king being commemorated on rock stella near Aswan and Nubia.

Amenhotep III has the distinction of having the most surviving statues of any Egyptian pharaoh, with over 250 having been discovered and identified. Since these statues span his entire life, they provide a series of portraits covering the entire length of his reign.

His enormous mortuary temple on the west bank of the Nile was, at the time, the largest complex in Thebes, but unfortunately he chose to build it too close to the floodplain and less than two hundred years later, it stood in ruins with 'The Colossi of Memnon' the only elements left standing.

When Amenhotep III died, he left behind a country that was at the very height of its power and influence, commanding immense respect in the international world, a position he had maintained largely through diplomacy and intermarriage with the royal families of other countries. Amenhotep III was buried in the Valley of the Kings, in Tomb KV22. His wife, Tiy, lived twelve years after his death. An examination of his mummy concluded that the pharaoh was aged between forty and fifty years old at death. His eldest son, Prince Tuthmoses had died before him, therefore it was his second son who inherited the throne upon his death. Amenhotep IV initially ruled using his own given royal name before changing it to Akhenaton - a name now synonymous with monotheism, (the belief in one god) and an age of religious revolution in ancient Egypt.

OPET FESTIVAL AT LUXOR TEMPLE:

The Temple of Luxor was the focus of one of the most important yearly New Kingdom celebrations, 'The Festival of Opet' when the god Amun and his consort, the goddess Mut, were reunited within the sanctuary of the temple. This festival translated as 'The Festival of the Secret Chamber' was celebrated in the second month of Akhet, the season of the flooding of the river and was linked to fertility and renewal.

The festival celebrates the birthday of the Kingly Ka, when the King got his Divine Right to rule, re-confirmed. The festival lasted many days, from eleven at the time of Tuthmoses III, to twenty-eight days during the reign of Ramses III.

Inundation was the time when people did not have a great workload, as it was long past harvest time and not yet time to plough and sow, therefore it was the ideal time for the celebration. During the festivities it's reported that thousands of loaves and hundreds of jars of beer were distributed free to the masses.

66

The procession, which began at Karnak and ended at the temple of Luxor, was usually made by barge, on the River Nile. The whole Theban triad of Amun, Mut and Khonsu, veiled from public view, and accompanied by pharaoh, were towed southward on their bark, either by boats under sail or by men with ropes along the shoreline. The procession was followed by dignitaries, dancers, singers, musicians, soldiers, and large crowds of common people. Priests carried incense, sistra were shaken by the female performers and there was great gaiety with singing and clapping of hands by everyone. All along the way there would have been merchants and peddlers offering wares to the people gathered on the shores waiting to catch sight of the barges.

When the barges stopped at several points along the river the people were encouraged to come forward and ask questions which could be answered with a simple 'yes' or 'no'. The priests would then cleverly tip the barge forward for 'yes' and backwards for 'no' as they saw fit.

Once they arrived at Luxor, the gods would be greeted by temple officials, acrobats, performing musicians and high dignitaries who sacrificed animals. From here the King, along with the statues and chief priests, disappeared inside the inner chambers where Amun, Mut and Khonsu were brought to their respective shrines. Not all the rituals which were performed inside the temple are known but there appears to have been a celebration of the sacred marriage between Amun and Mut in order to certify the ruling pharaoh as a true son of the gods.

The festival was a renewal of the King's right to rule and served once again to confirm him as a divine being, a living god on Earth.

The crowd outside, who anxiously awaited the transformed king, would cheer wildly at he re-emerged. The festival was the backbone of pharaoh's power and the greatest Theban festival during the whole year.

HISTORY OF THE SPHINX

The Sphinx is a mystical beast portrayed with the head of a man and the body of a lion and is shown wearing the royal head cloth (Nemes) of Pharaoh. In ancient times the Sphinx would have been brightly coloured. The origins of the word are debatable. In ancient Greek the word sphinx means; 'strangler'. The Arabs call it, 'Abu Hol', meaning; 'The Father of Terror'. However some believe that the name may have come from the Egyptian phrase 'shesep ankh', which means 'living image'. The sphinx was associated with both pharaoh and the sun-god, Ra and in the New Kingdom also 'Horem akhet', Horus in the Horizon'. (Horus is often seen as the son of Ra.). The Great Sphinx at the pyramid site measures 73m long and has a maximum height of 20m and is considered to be the; 'Guardian of the Necropolis of Giza'.

Quite likely you will round this trip off with a visit to one of Luxor's papyrus galleries. Here you may be given a demonstration of how real papyrus is made and how not to fall victim to the 'banana-leaf' sellers. And just to make sure you don't, they will have a large collection of authentic papyrus for you to browse through and hopefully purchase. Other non-ancient trips during your cruise may include; Alabaster Workshop, Silk Factory, Bazaar, or Perfumery.

Again the trip to the two temples will involve an early start and will take about three to four hours, by which time you will probably be ready for lunch. If your cruise is following this common schedule you are probably asking yourself, 'When on earth are we actually going to set sail?' as by now you will have been on the boat for two days and not moved an inch! But don't despair; as the chances are you should set sail that very afternoon, maybe even as you are enjoying your lunch. Then, as the industrial suburbs of Luxor finally give way to the wide open views of the river and countryside, you at last feel as if you are on a cruise. This is when you really get a sense of what life must have been like, as you can almost imagine yourself being transported back in time to when Pharaohs sailed the River Nile.

Passing through Esna Lock

At some stage during the evening, usually after dinner, the boat passes through the Esna lock and moors up at the town of Edfu. More than likely your cruise boat will have to queue to get through the lock and this is the time when opportunistic local boatmen surround the cruise ships in order to peddle their wares, day or night, which they do by shouting to anyone stood on the deck.

Then, once they get your attention, they start throwing goods up from some twenty feet below, mostly linen products; table cloths, towel, sheets, napkins, etc.

Items start going everywhere, on top of sun awnings, into the pool, on tables, chairs and all the time these tradesmen will be haggling madly with anyone who is willing to listen. Then, if a price is finally agreed the man will throw up a weighted pouch for the customer to put their money in.

This all sounds very friendly and a bit of fun, and for the most part it is. However this is not a game to these men, this is how they earn their living and they will attempt to get a sale anyway they can. (I will refer to Esna Lock and the boatmen again in the 'Telling You How It Is' section.)

Once again there will probably be some form of entertainment later in the evening. Quite commonly the captain will hold a small cocktail party where the management of the boat and your travel guides are introduced to everyone.

DAY THREE:

Today you will probably visit the Temple of Horus in Edfu. Once again this is likely to involve an early start, something you are probably getting used to by now, as sleep is obviously not a high priority on a Nile cruise! ☺

Photography is allowed both inside and outside of the temple. Depending on numbers, this journey involves a five to ten minute drive in a horse-drawn caleshe, taxi, or privately hired mini bus or coach. Generally speaking your tour will last for approximately two hours at the end of which you may have a group photograph taken. One of the most popular spots for this is between the two large stone Horus statues in the main courtyard. The local photographer will deliver the photos to the boat later when you will have a chance to purchase a copy. Visitors to the temple are given their guided tour outside and inside.

Just outside of the temple there is a large local market where you may be given some time to explore and practise your haggling skills. And maybe even pick up a few bargains! But don't get too carried away as haggling can be a lengthy process and the tour group will not be too pleased if you're back late. If you aren't interested in purchasing anything then it's best to avoid making eye contact with any trader and simply make your way back to your coach.

EDFU TEMPLE

This Ptolemaic temple is the best conserved of all Egyptian temples and is almost in a perfect state of preservation with some of the roofs still surviving. Despite its fairly recent age (only 2000 years old) Edfu still reflects traditional pharaonic architecture, giving us an excellent example of how all temples once looked.

Edfu is also the second largest temple in Egypt, after Karnak. Built of sandstone it is the only temple to be situated on the west bank of the Nile, some 60 miles south of Luxor. Dedicated to the deity Horus, it was home to several festivals sacred to the said god. The best documented was where an image of Hathor (Horus' wife) was taken on an elaborate trip from her place of residence at Dendera to Edfu.

The magnificent Edfu Temple

Horus harpooning the hippo

Part of the Naos (Sanctuary) at Edfu

Work began on the temple in 237 BC and took twenty five years to complete. Further work was carried out between the years 140-71

BC with a larger 18 columned hypostyle hall, forecourt, enclosure wall and a 37 metre high pylon being added at various stages. The original work was started by Ptolemy III (Greek Ruler) and carried on through numerous reigns until Ptolemy XII, with the actual doors of the pylon not being hung until 51 BC; some 186 years after building first began. The nucleus of the temple (the naos) consists of a sanctuary, a twelve columned hypostyle hall and numerous vestibules, small chapels and chambers. The sacred sanctuary holds a shrine and a replica of an ancient barge. This area was known as the inner sanctum, which in ancient times was only accessible to Pharaoh and the highest-ranking priests. Here the sacred statue of the god would reside to whom daily homage was given by way of food, chant and prayer.

What has disappeared from the temple over the centuries are the auxiliary buildings which included kitchens, abattoirs, storerooms, administrative offices, all of which are now buried under the modern day town of Edfu, along with the sacred lake and groves. The original obelisks have also long disappeared.

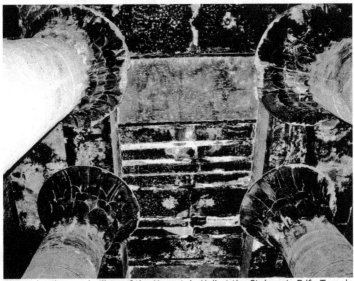

Charred ceiling and pillars of the Hypostyle Hall at the Ptolemaic Edfu Temple

The temple is orientated south to north in alignment with Orion and the Great Bear constellations. Decoration, reliefs and inscriptions in the temple consist of the mythology of Horus, Hathor and their child, Ihy. (The Edfu Triad) You can see an example of this on the walls of the Ambulatory where Horus is shown slaying the evil god, Seth, who has taken on the guise of a hippopotamus which lurks beneath his boat.

71

Close by, on the east side corridor, you will find access to the Nilometer where temple priests tallied tithes based on Nile water levels.

EDFU TEMPLE

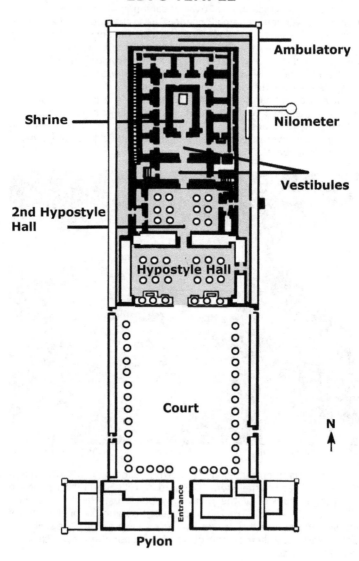

In later years Egyptians ceased using the temple for religious purposes and during the roman occupation of Egypt, Christians took over the temple for daily living. You can see visible evidence of this in the blackened ceiling of the hypostyle hall which is believed to have been caused either by regular building of fires, or the result of arson intended to destroy religious imagery that was then considered pagan.

ALEXANDER THE GREAT AND PTOLEMY PERIOD:

By 330 B.C. Egypt had been occupied for nearly two hundred years by Persia who had incorporated it into its own growing empire. The Persian rulers assumed the Egyptian crown by right of conquest, exploited its vast grain reserves, taxed its people heavily and showed little respect for the ancient traditions. Therefore when Alexander the Great advanced into Egypt in late 332 BC he was regarded more as a saviour and liberator, than a conqueror.

As the Egyptian people's choice he was offered the double crown of the Two Lands and was anointed as pharaoh in Memphis on 14 November 332 BC, with the culmination of his coronation being the climactic moment when the high priest named him 'son of the gods' according to traditions dating back almost 3,000 years.

Alexander was so struck by Egypt and her people's beliefs that from that moment onwards he often referred to Zeus-Amun as being his true father and reinforced this belief by having himself adorned with ram horns, as a symbol of his divinity and godly association with Amun, on any subsequently minted coinage.

As a devout man Alexander had no difficulty worshipping the Egyptian deities and equated their gods with his own, worshipping Amun as a form of Zeus.

During his stay in Egypt, he founded Alexandria-by-Egypt, which would become the prosperous capital of the Ptolemaic kingdom after his death. Alexander left Egypt in the early part of 331 BC a changed man and although he would never return alive to see the city he had founded, it is widely believed that Alexandria was his final resting place when his embalmed body was returned there for burial some 10 years later. (It should be stated though, that as of yet no tomb has been found, but documentary evidence is strong.)

The Ptolemaic dynasty was a Greek royal family which ruled the Ptolemaic Empire in Egypt during the Hellenistic period. Their rule in Egypt lasted some 300 years, from 332 BC to 31 BC. Ptolemy served with Alexander the Great and it was he who was appointed one of the governors of Egypt after Alexander's death in 323 BC. Eighteen years later in 304 BC he went on to declare himself King Ptolemy I of Egypt, a position the Egyptians accepted, as they saw the Ptolemies as the natural successors to the pharaohs of an independent Egypt. The Ptolemies rule was very successful until the Roman conquest of 31 BC.

All the male rulers of the dynasty took the name Ptolemy. Ptolemaic queens, some of whom were the sisters of their husbands, included Queen Cleopatra VII. Cleopatra was famously known for the part she played in the Roman political battles between Julius Caesar and the Roman Senate, and later between Octavian and her Roman lover, Mark Antony. Her suicide marked the end of Ptolemaic rule in Egypt and the beginning of Roman government. During Cleopatra's reign the population of Egypt was seven million and it was the richest country on the Mediterranean.

When you return, your afternoon will probably be spent relaxing on the sundeck or in your room whilst the boat sets sail for Kom Ombo, some 33 miles south of Edfu. Depending on your schedule you may end up visiting Komombo soon after arrival, which will involve a mid-afternoon tour. Luckily not many site visits take place during the hottest part of the day, but if this does happen at Komombo make sure you wear plenty of sun cream. Also carry a supply of bottled water as the heat can become quite overbearing with a danger of dehydration. Photography is allowed throughout the temple. The visit will take approximately 2 hours.

KOM OMBO TEMPLE:

The mirror image temples at Kom Ombo. Right Sobek's temple, left Horus'

Another Ptolemaic temple, Kom Ombo, which means the 'Mound of Ombo', stands on a promontory in a bend of the Nile whose scouring currents washed away parts of the temple many centuries ago. Even so the site is still remarkably well preserved and its reliefs amongst some of the best in Egypt, with a quantity of the artwork still retaining its brilliant colours.

74

The temple is quite exceptional in that it is dedicated equally to two deities and as such is actually two temples that run adjacent and parallel to each other. The left side of the temple was consecrated to Horus, whilst the right was devoted to the crocodile god, Sobek. Both shared equal honours and a double worship, which is a unique unification in Ancient Egypt.

KOM OMBO TEMPLE

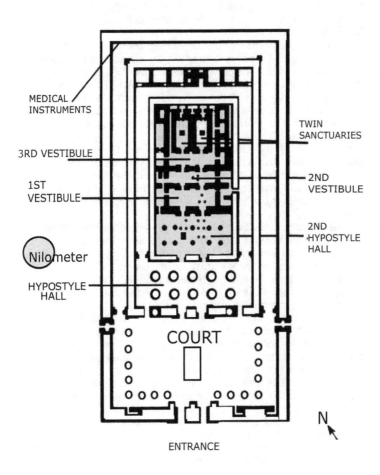

MEDICAL INSTRUMENTS

TWIN SANCTUARIES

3RD VESTIBULE

2ND VESTIBULE

1ST VESTIBULE

2ND HYPOSTYLE HALL

Nilometer

HYPOSTYLE HALL

COURT

N

ENTRANCE

The temples are the same in all senses, with two of everything; gateways, chapels, hypostyle halls, inner sanctums and shrines with an imaginary line drawn along the axis dividing it into two symmetrical halves. The ruined sanctuaries of the two gods stand side by side and in each you can see the granite plinths that supported the sacred barques that were paraded during festivals. It's believed that there may have been two separate priesthoods working in the temple, each making duplicate offerings to the two divine triads that grace the walls in ritual scenes. The triads consisted of Horus, Tasentnefert and their son Panebtawi and Sobek, Hathor and their son Khonsu. (In ancient Egyptian mythology gods and goddesses relationships often overlapped and intertwined) The individual temples were called the 'House of the Crocodile' and 'Castle of the Falcon'.

The temple's construction began during the reign of Ptolemy V (205-180 BC) and was continued on by others until Ptolemy XII (80-51 BC), who was responsible for most of the decoration. After the Roman invasion, Emperor Tiberius (AD 14-37) built and decorated the forecourt, followed by subsequent Roman rulers who continued to add various decorative works, ending with Macrinus (217-218 AD). Therefore the building of Kom Ombo took some 400 years, over twice as long as that of Edfu!

The columns of the hypostyle hall are noted for their elegant foliage capitals and on the northern wall of the ambulatory are reliefs which are believed to be the first representations of surgical instruments in Egypt, including, scalpels, forceps, medicine bottles and scissors. Kom Ombo is the only known temple to show medical reliefs.

On the opposite wall, part way up, you will see a small false door surrounded by hearing ears and sacred eyes through which the priests would deliver oracles to the people waiting outside the main part of the temple. Unbeknown to the crowds the priests would use a secret staircase and concealed from view they would answer any questions put to them making the people think that the gods themselves were actually speaking to them.

Until late in the 1900s the area around Kom Ombo was infested with crocodiles and so in ancient times the people thought to placate them by honouring Sobek, to whom crocodiles were sacred. It's also thought that the priests may have bred them in a small pool on the western side of the temple. For many years the temple housed a crocodile museum which contained several mummified crocodiles and sarcophagi found during excavations carried out in the nearby necropolis area, however they were removed in 2009, so I'm sorry to say there are no more 'real' crocs to see at Kom Ombo, only those carved on the walls.

To the left of the temple there is also another Nilometer used to measure the level of the river waters.

Falcon-headed Horus and Crocodile-headed Sobek at Kom Ombo

The all seeing, all listening wall at Kom Ombo

Nilometer – you can see the spiralling steps used by the priests in ancient times to check Nile water levels.

Remains of a granite plinth

Medical instruments

A decorative frieze of cobras runs along the upper part of a wall

The cobra was an important snake in Ancient Egypt and was seen as the protector of pharaoh. (You can read more about the cobra's role in the Egyptian Mythology section.)

After your tour of Kom Ombo ends, you will probably be left to make your own way back to the boat, which will be moored only a short walking distance away. To do this you will be directed out of the temple via a route that will force you to pass through the market stalls, so be prepared for the usual hassle, which I'm sure you are getting very accustomed to, even if it is still annoying. ☺
A tip, as the men continue to try and sell you their goods just remember to keep walking as the price is likely to drop the closer you get to your boat and their desperation increases to make a sale. One note of warning, if you handle the goods, i.e. put them on, open them up, then the sellers are more likely to try to pressurise you into making a purchase.
During dinner the boat will probably set sail for Aswan, which is the furthest south the cruise ship will travel.
This will be the start of a two-day stay in Aswan, which is situated some 81 miles south of Luxor. As you travelled south you will notice it's been getting hotter and as Egypt's sunniest city it isn't unusual for Aswan to be anything from four to eight degrees hotter than Luxor.

DAY FOUR
ASWAN (Ancient Egyptian name; Syene)
UNFINISHED OBELISK
Usually the first day starts around 7am with a 10 minute trip by coach to the old granite quarries at Aswan, where a 137 foot

unfinished obelisk weighing over 1150 tons lies abandoned due to a crack. The incident happened some 3000 years ago when stonemasons were working on the monument and a large fissure developed. Hewn directly out of the bedrock, cracks appeared in the granite obelisk and the project was abandoned. The bottom side is still attached to the bedrock.

Nearly one third larger than any other ancient Egyptian obelisk ever erected, the unfinished obelisk is the biggest known. Unfortunately the commissioner of the obelisk is unknown, but archeologists have speculated that it was intended for Karnak Temple, with possible contenders being Pharaohs; Hatshepsut, Tuthmoses III or Ramses the Great.

Dolomite rocks were used to work granite

Chisel marks left by ancient tools.

The unfinished obelisk, discovered in 1922 by Egyptologist Rex Engelbach, offers unusual insights into ancient Egyptian masonry techniques, with marks from workers tools still clearly visible.

The basic shape of the obelisk was created by workers pounding out the shape using dolomite rocks which are harder than granite and creating a one meter trench around the perimeter in the shape of the obelisk. Engelbach estimated that at any one time 130 men would be working the obelisk, each in a space about four feet square.

Much of the red granite used for ancient temples and colossi came from quarries in the Aswan area and being so close to the Nile meant that the granite blocks could be loaded on to boats and shipped downstream to the building sites. Reliefs depicting the transportation of an obelisk can be found in Hatshepsut's mortuary temple at Deir el Bahri. It is also documented that it took about seven months to construct an obelisk.

Unfinished obelisk as seen from its square base and pyramidal top

All the ancient quarries at Aswan are classed as 'open air museums' and as such are officially protected by the Egyptian government as archeological sites of great importance. The unfinished obelisk location has recently been revamped and equipped with tourist facilities in order to attract more visitors to the Aswan area.

There are no restrictions on photography or video.

HIGH DAM

From the quarry you will be taken to see the High Dam, which controls the Nile and is the major source of hydroelectric power in Egypt. Your guide may warn you against taking photographs in this

81

sensitive area. The area actually has two dams, the Old Aswan Dam which was built by British engineers between 1898 and 1902 and the second, larger High Dam, some 7 km further upriver, built by the Russians between 1960 and 1971.

The old British dam, designed as a gravity-buttress dam was opened yearly to allow nutrient-rich silt water through in a controlled way so as to not to cause flooding, but did not retain water. The dam was raised twice in order to cope with the annual flooding but eventually a new one had to be built.

Unlike the old dam, the High Dam does capture the Nile floodwater in the world's third largest reservoir, Lake Nasser, and releases it as required. Unfortunately, along with the good benefits, the dam has also produced several negative side effects.

The British Old Dam still produces electricity and the lock is still working

In order to build the dam thousands of Egyptian Nubians had to leave their land with many homes, artefacts, religious centres and cemeteries being lost forever beneath the water. Plus, the rich silt that normally fertilized the land during the annual flood is now stuck at the bottom of Lake Nasser, forcing Egyptian farmers to use a million tons of artificial fertilizer as a substitute for the natural nutrients. This lack of natural fertilizer has resulted in increased erosion of the river and a promotion of dangerous algae and algal blooms which affects fish stocks. Also because of the build-up of silt in the lake there has been an increase in the growth of plant life in the lake's stagnant waters which supports the snails that carry the debilitating disease schistosomiasis (also known as bilharzias or snail fever), which means the lake has to be periodically dredged and the water cleaned to prevent disease, which is all very expensive. Navigation of the Nile has also been compromised, as unlike the British Old Dam, which has a lock, the Russian's High Dam does not.

On the positive side, the Aswan High Dam has increased the quality of life of millions of Egyptians by stopping the annual flooding which ruined so many livelihoods and claimed lives. Also the lake provided the ideal conditions for the Nile crocodile whose population bounced back with its creation, after being on the verge of extinction. Today, some 40 years since the High Dam's inauguration, official government census estimates the number of Nile crocodiles in Lake Nasser to be around 5,000. Plus the dam's 12 turbines generate over 10 billion kilowatts of electricity every year, providing 90% of Egypt's electrical power, with the other 10% coming from the Esna lock. However as energy demands increase there are plans to construct several power plants at various locations. With the World Bank allocating a $270 million loan, Egypt's government is now intensely focusing on solar energy technologies with an aim to generate 20% of its electricity output from renewable sources by 2020 and to triple the current capacity by 2027. These plans include the building of a solar power technology plant near Kom Ombo. Construction is scheduled to start in 2012 and hopes are that it will be fully functional by 2016. There are also plans to construct four 250 MW wind farm plants on the Red Sea coast at Gabal el-Zeit.

The embankment High Dam built by Russians

PHILAE TEMPLE

You will finish your day's outing at the Greco-Roman Temple of Philae dedicated to the goddess Isis. Once you disembark from your coach the temple is reached via a short boat ride. Quite often children also get onto the ferryboats trying to sell cheap souvenirs to the tourists, such as beaded necklaces and arm bracelets of Nubian design. Some are quite pretty, but don't expect them to last.

The temple was submerged for most of the year when the first dam was completed in 1902 and after the erection of the High Dam the island was left surrounded by swirling waters that threatened its destruction. So an international decision was taken to save the temple before its recovery became impossible. Even so it still took another eight years, from 1972 to 1980, before the temple was dismantled stone by stone from its original position on Philae Island and reassembled on Agilqiyyah Island. Firstly a cofferdam was put around the temple and the water drained away. They then cut the temple up into manageable blocks, numbering each one as they went along. Then each block was injected with a special resin that hardened and stopped them from crumbling due to years of water damage. Next steel rods were inserted to help with reconstruction. Whilst this was taking place Agilqiyyah was cut down and completely reshaped to imitate Philae Island as closely as possible. The whole project was a massive and very complicated piece of engineering. In the picture below all that's left to see of Philae Island are a few jutting metal girders that formed part of the cofferdam.

There are no photography or video restrictions at the site.

Metal posts the only visual remains of Philae Island as seen from Agilqiyyah

Philae temple was devoted to the cult of the goddess Isis and according to legend also the final burial place of her husband, Osiris, the Underworld god. (You can read the full story in the Egyptian Mythology section.)

Work was begun on the temple by Nectanebo I (380-362 BC) and continued under the Ptolemies, with a graceful pavilion being added by the roman Emperor Trajan. The entrance is near a porch built by Nectanebo I and leads through into the area known as the Eastern and Western colonnades. The western is the most complex and complete with the eastern never being finished and many of the capitals are blank.

At the southern end is a small temple of Arensnuphis, a late Nubian deity. The first pylon was built by Ptolemies XII (80-51 BC) and XIII (51-47 BC). Two obelisks that used to stand in front of the pylons are now in Dorset. On the east side at right angles to the main temple is the gateway of Ptolemy II (284-246 BC). Beyond the pylon is the first court and on the west side is the mammisi (Birth House) with a columned forecourt, two vestibules and a sanctuary showing the birth scenes of the child Horus.

On the north side of the first court is the second pylon built by Ptolemy VIII (170-116 BC) and decorated by Ptolemy XIII. The main temple of Isis lies behind the pylon and consists of a columned hall, beyond which lies three vestibules that lead to the sanctuary.

Philae is yet another temple that was occupied by Christians. Reliefs in the hypostyle hall were damaged when the temple was turned into a church in the 6th Century AD.

The temple was originally surrounded by a town but the mud-brick houses disappeared many centuries ago.

Philae Temple, as seen on approach from the motorboat

Christian (Coptic) altar with cross situated in Philae's main Hypostyle Hall

85

Rods inserted into stones to help lock them in place during rebuild

The Kiosk of Trajan

The most important buildings outside of the temple are the Hathor Temple built by Ptolemy VII and south of this is the famous Kiosk of Trajan, built around 100 AD and once called 'Pharaoh's Bed' with its rectangular chamber surrounded by 14 beautiful columns with composite capitals. (See below)

PHILAE

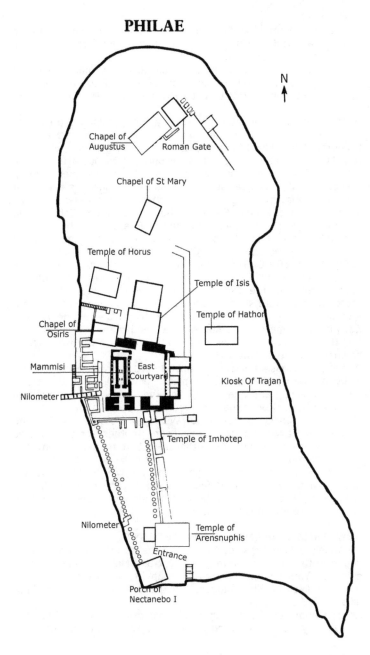

N

Chapel of Augustus

Roman Gate

Chapel of St Mary

Temple of Horus

Temple of Isis

Temple of Hathor

Chapel of Osiris

Mammisi

East Courtyard

Nilometer

Kiosk Of Trajan

Temple of Imhotep

Nilometer

Temple of Arensnuphis

Entrance

Porch of Nectanebo I

PERFUMERY

Besides the normal sightseeing venues your guide may also take you to a local perfumery where they manufacture oriental perfumes, flower oils and blends. Oils in Aswan are far cheaper than in Luxor, or Cairo. As all these oils are 100% natural without alcohol or water to dilute them, so they are fresh, strong, not overly-sweet and certainly last longer as you are buying pure essence.

Upon entering an Egyptian perfumery the guests are presented with a list of the various products they sell and offered a drink while the factory guide explains the list of aromas. Jars of oil are passed around and the guest is encouraged to put a drop on a small area of the arm, rub it and smell it. Besides the beautiful scents of flower essences such as Lotus Flower, Jasmine and Violet you can choose from the more exotic name of the essence blends such as Scent of Arabia, Secret of the Desert, Queen Nefertiti and Harem. They can also make up famous international brands. For example in 2011 a 50ml bottle of 'Five Secrets', their equivalent of Channel No 5, will cost you 200LE, a 100ml bottle 300LE and a 300ml bottle 600LE. Therefore if you have a favourite expensive perfume, ask about it, test it, and cost it up against the price you normally pay for the same amount, as it may well save you a pretty penny. These shops are fixed price, so no haggling involved. Although some of the prices may seem steep it's worth noting that Egyptian perfume oils are not exported and therefore you will not find them on the shelves of your local store. So if you want some, be sure to buy them there.

Perfumes and essential oils have been used for thousands of years in Egypt, with plants and their parts being utilised in the art of healing, relaxing and energizing. And today they are still made in much the same way as they were during pharaonic time.

TIP: When buying perfume, always make sure you watch the retailer decant the one you have chosen! In other words ask to see the order being made up, do not let them take the bottle away into a back room out of sight.

TIP: If you are prepared to haggle than you will get the perfumes even cheaper away from the factory shop, but this could be difficult considering you are on a tight schedule and opportunities to explore on your own is limited.

HOW PERFUME WAS MADE IN ANCIENT EGYPT:

It's widely believed that perfumery, or the art of making perfumes, began in the ancient cultures of Egypt and Mesopotamia. Pictorial evidence from Egyptian tombs and papyrus and written evidence from the likes of Pliny suggest that perfume was made in three different ways.

As distillation for the extraction of essences was unknown to the Ancient Egyptians, they used either oil or animal fats to create the strong smelling perfumes. The most common basic oil used was castor oil.

The first technique was 'enfleurage', when flowers, fruits or seeds were soaked in layers of oil or fat. This steeping produced creams and pomades for the skin and hair. Pomades were frequently worn at banqueting scenes by both sexes. As the wax cones melted they gave off a pleasant smell. These would be renewed by servants who carried replacements on a tray.

The second process 'maceration' created perfume by dipping crushed flowers, herbs etc into oil that was then heated to around 65 degrees. The mixture was then sieved, cooled and poured into cosmetic vessels.

The third process was the expressing of flowers, seeds etc which were put into a bag with sticks attached to both ends. The sticks were then twisted in opposite directions to exert pressure to produce the essential oils. This method was the least favoured.

Recent news revealed that scientists are trying to re-create the favourite perfume of Egyptian Queen Hatshepsut from a 3,500 year old perfume bottle that was found amongst the queen's possessions. X-rays revealed that the bottle still contains residue and scientists plan to identify the substance from the remnants of the ancient oil and possibly, within a year, re-create it. It will be fascinating to see if they can manage to manufacture the fragrance.

A perfumed cone placed on top of head. All classes wore them.

The whole morning trip, including perfumery will last approximately 4-5 hours.

FELUCCA RIDE

On your return to the cruise boat the tour representative may have arranged a felucca ride for you and your fellow companions to Kitcheners Island and its botanical gardens, or maybe just a scenic sail up and down the Nile and around Elephantine Island and the First Cataract. A felucca is a lovely way to travel the river and take in some of the sites.

Legend has it that the 'Ark of the Covenant' was once brought to Elephantine Island by Jewish priests escaping persecution by King Manasseh of Israel. It's said that whilst on the island they built a Jewish temple in 650 B.C. which served as a resting place for the Ark for 200 years. The ancient Elephantine Papyri seem to confirm the existence of a Jewish Temple on the island. The legend continues that the Ark was eventually taken further up the Nile River to its eventual resting place in the remote highlands of the ancient land of Kush, modern day Ethiopia. People still make pilgrimages to the island. Other attractions on the island include Nilometer, Temples of Khnum and Satat and several Nubian villages. If you get chance it's also a good place to spend some leisure time.

The Movenpick Hotel on Elephantine Island

At some stage the owner of the felucca may lay out his wares for you to look at, which usually consists of some arts and crafts, plus jewellery. You will find this happens on most of the boat trips you take, as they never like to miss out on an opportunity to sell to a captive audience. ☺ Sometimes you also find young boys paddling up to the feluccas in homemade canoes and asking for money or pens. I usually photograph them for 1LE each.

Don't forget to take your camera for those beautiful Nile shots and offshore pictures of your cruise boat. The sail will last about an hour.

90

Noble tombs as seen from the Nile at Aswan

In the evening there will probably be an opportunity for you to revisit Philae Temple for the Sound and Light Show. You watch the first part of the show in different parts of the temple, including the colonnade area. Then you are taken to seats in the auditorium for the remainder. It's quite enjoyable but I think the latter half goes on a little too long. If you've already seen the Karnak show then I wouldn't bother.

As you are now in the old Nubian region of Ancient Egypt the evening onboard entertainment could be authentic Nubian Dancers, folk group or musicians.

ASWAN CITY
Out and About:
Aswan is Egypt's southern most city on the First Cataract. Here the river is strewn with boulders and rocks which make the river unnavigable, so this is as far as your cruise ship can go.
Aswan is a frontier town where the Middle East meets Africa. The town is small enough to walk around and graced with the most beautiful setting on the Nile. Any spare time can be spent strolling up and down the Corniche watching the sailboats gracefully glide over the Nile with their tall masts etched against a blue sky. Or you could sit in a floating restaurant eating freshly cooked food whilst listening to the rhythmic drum beat of Nubian music.
Then later why not view the spectacular sunsets while having tea on the terrace of the Old Cataract Hotel and enter the world of legendary people and stories. The hotel was built the banks of the Nile, opposite Elephantine Island, by the English in 1898. Majestically positioned on a granite shelf it overlooks the Nile at

the First Cataract, hence its name. With its Victorian facade, the hotel retains all its original beauty including period rooms, polished marble floors and classic Islamic arches. Note: The hotel has been closed since May 2008 for renovations but is due to reopen in September this year, 2011, under the name of 'Sofitel Legend Old Cataract'.

The Nile at Aswan is at its most beautiful, flowing through ochre desert, steely granite rocks, and round emerald islands covered in palm groves and tropical plants.

The Old Cataract Hotel where Agatha Christie stayed

Aswan is famous for its spices, Nubian artwork, jewellery, perfumes, scarves and baskets. Spices in particular are far cheaper than at Luxor. For example spices that will cost you 10LE in Luxor, you'll get for 4LE in Aswan. The price of a return taxi from your boat to the local souq (market) for a one hour shop should cost you around 50LE.

Since construction of the Aswan Dam the city has become an important industrial centre for steel, aluminium and chemical industries.

Unlike Luxor, Aswan has a far more distinct African feel to it and its popularity has grown over the past decade. A fact reflected in the price of land that was 10LE a square metre in 2000 and is now 900LE a square metre in 2011. These days it is fondly referred to as the 'Egyptian Riviera'.

Other extra excursions you may like to consider are;

CITY TOUR OF ASWAN

This tour involves a visit to a mosque in the oldest part of the city, a trip to a high point which affords you a panoramic view of Aswan and a visit to a local market where you can haggle for some cheap gifts, such as spices, leather goods and hand-made Nubian jewellery. To round your trip off you may meet up with your guide at a coffee shop where you can sample the local brew. The trip usually takes place late afternoon and gets you back just in time for your evening meal.

NUBIAN VILLAGE

Take a leisurely sail up the Nile to a Nubian village.

Aswan has become the permanent home of the 5000 year old civilisation and the vast majority of people living in Aswan are Nubians. Their villages have a distinctive African atmosphere.

The building of the Nasser Dam at Aswan spelt disaster for the Nubians. Their homeland was flooded and the people dispersed to different parts of the country or resettled in villages on higher ground. Their way of life never recovered with families being scattered throughout the region. The houses provided were smaller and life became much noisier, crowded and busier than it used to be. Many customs are also being lost like traditional Nubian jewellery design and women's traditional costume, with the younger generation preferring to dress like the modern Cairo or European woman.

How they earn a living has also changed. Traditionally Nubians were famers but when they lost their land the men had to turn to work in the tourist industry as felucca and motorboat operators, hotel workers, waiters or cruise ship staff. This makes them heavily reliant on the tourists for an income. If you get the chance, speak with some of the village elders to get a real insight as to what life was really like before the dam.

ASWAN

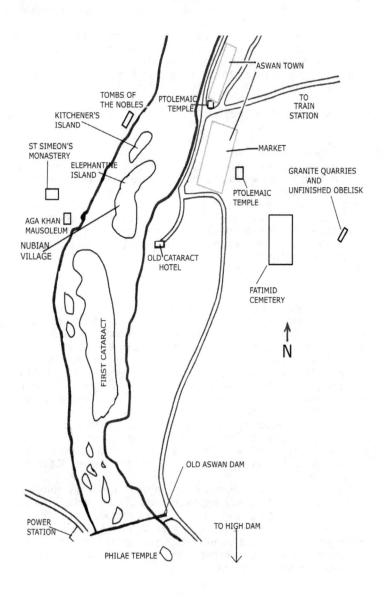

- ASWAN TOWN
- TO TRAIN STATION
- TOMBS OF THE NOBLES
- PTOLEMAIC TEMPLE
- KITCHENER'S ISLAND
- ST SIMEON'S MONASTERY
- MARKET
- ELEPHANTINE ISLAND
- GRANITE QUARRIES AND UNFINISHED OBELISK
- PTOLEMAIC TEMPLE
- AGA KHAN MAUSOLEUM
- NUBIAN VILLAGE
- OLD CATARACT HOTEL
- FATIMID CEMETERY
- N
- FIRST CATARACT
- OLD ASWAN DAM
- POWER STATION
- TO HIGH DAM
- PHILAE TEMPLE

DAY FIVE
This day will either be spent at your own leisure, i.e., sightseeing, sunbathing or shopping. Other places of interest around Aswan include the Nubian Museum, Tombs of the Nobles, temples of Kalabsha, Dedwen, Gerf Hussein, Beit el-Wali, the Kiosk of Qertassi, the Monastery of St Simeon, and the Aga Khan Mausoleum. (No longer allowed inside)

Kalabshe Temple (Kiosk of Qertassi to left) as seen from the High Dam

There is also a Palace of Culture, where the artists perform Nubian stick dancing and sing folk songs about their village life.
Alternatively, what most people do on their first visit is sign up for an optional excursion, the most popular being a trip to the Temples at Abu Simbel. If within your budget, I strongly urge you to take this trip.

ABU SIMBEL TOUR
Abu Simbel is a village lying 174 miles (280 km) south of Aswan and only 25 miles (40 km) north of the Sudanese border. It is a very small settlement with very little to attract visitors other than its great temples for which it is famous. Few tourists linger for more than a few hours. You will probably be given the choice of travelling either by coach or plane to the site.
By far the most popular, due to cost, is the daily police escorted coach option. The trip takes roughly three hours through the desert and usually involves a stop off to photograph the sunrise. On the return journey you may stop again, this time to get the chance to ride a camel. If you are travelling on one of the larger air-conditioned coaches there may be a small toilet on board, which to be honest, is probably best avoided if at all possible. Abu Simbel via coach is definitely not a trip I would recommend if you were suffering from any form of stomach bug or diarrhoea. Those taking the coach are woken around 3.15am am and taken to the assembly point. The convoy usually consists of 30-40 coaches and once they start they don't hang around, racing through the desert. Before leaving you will have been issued with a packed breakfast, which you can enjoy on the journey.
By comparison the plane trip will take approximately 35 minutes. Also you will have the advantage of being the first visitors of the day, when the site is cooler and easier to get around, plus you're back hours before the coach travellers. Obviously the downside is the cost and the trip can be subject to cancellation if there are not enough participants.

95

There is a Sound and Light show every evening at Abu Simbel, which I have been told is the best in Egypt; however as cruisers you won't get the chance to see it, as your visit will take place early in the morning.

ABU SIMBEL TEMPLES
The most remarkable Nubian antiquities are the 3000 year old temples at Abu Simbel. Built by Pharaoh Ramses II around 1250-1269 BC, he dedicated one of the temples to himself and the other to his wife, Nefertari. These temples are unique because they were originally hewn out of the sandstone cliff, as opposed to being built stone by stone.

The huge colossi of Ramses Temple

For centuries the larger of the temples was lost, hidden under a huge blanket of sand blown off the western desert and it wasn't until John Lewis Burckhardt, a 19th century traveller, was visiting the smaller temple that he noticed the tops of four colossal statues. It would then be another two years before the Egyptologist Belzoni arrived at the site and began the clearance.

In 1817 entrance was gained into the temple's interior.

The most impressive feature of Ramses temple is the four giant seated colossi statues which front the buildings, each measuring 66 feet high (20 metres). Internally there are two halls, a dozen chambers and a sanctuary. Abu Simbel was Ramses II greatest architectural project.

As with Philae, the building of the High Dam necessitated the dismantling and removal of the Abu Simbel temples. Thankfully this happened in the 1960's before submerging waters could cause any damage. Many ideas were considered, including surrounding the cliff with its own dam, another entailed viewing the temples through huge underwater domes and another favoured hydraulically lifting the temples centimetre by centimetre until they were above water level.

In the end they decided upon sawing the temples into 1041 blocks and moving them piecemeal to be reassembled on top of the plateau, some 200 feet higher and 700 feet away from their original site. This painstaking work was started in 1966, and mostly completed by 1968, with finishing touches being added in 1972. The work was carried out by engineers from many countries including Sweden, Italy, Germany, France and Egypt. Most of the joins in the stone have now been filled by antiquity experts, but inside the temples it is still possible to see where the blocks were cut. The total cost was put at around 17 million pounds sterling. Considering their size, it was one of the greatest engineering feats of modern times. The internal concrete and steel dome that now support the man-made hills and temples can be visited via a small entrance to the right of the huge Ramses colossi, subject to it being open.

The temple was dedicated to the gods Ptah, Amun-Ra, Re-Harakhte and the deified king himself. The axis of the temple was arranged so that at sunrise the rays of the sun penetrate the innermost sanctuary bathing the seated stone statues in light. Unfortunately when the temple was moved modern engineers were unable to recreate this effect due to angle deviation. The fact that the ancient Egyptians were capable of creating this stunning effect says an awful lot about their technical, constructive and mathematical abilities. The interior walls are decorated with the usual scenes of deity worship and kingly prowess in war, including Ramses most famous battle at Kadesh, against the Hittites.

The smaller of the temples is dedicated to the goddess Hathor and to the deified 'Great Consort' of Pharaoh, Nefertari. Six statutes front the entrance. They are smaller than the four colossi on Ramses temple, but nevertheless still impressive, as they appear to walk out of the cliff wall towards anyone who approaches. Four of the figures represent Ramses and the other two, Queen Nefertari. Smaller figures by their sides represent the sons and daughters of the royal couple. Although smaller, the interior design and decoration of Nefertari's temple, is, in some respects, more graceful than the masculinity of the king's temple, and therefore in my opinion, somewhat finer.

Tour guides are not allowed to give talks in either of the temples and once again there is no photography or video allowed internally, proving yet again the inconsistency of the Egyptian Authorities, who ban photography in one temple, but allow it in another. It really is annoying, especially as the cost of the extra excursion to Abu Simbel is not cheap!

I just count myself fortunate that I visited and photographed Abu Simbel, and other no-go areas many years ago, before these restrictions came into place.

ABU SIMBEL

Great Temple fo Ramses II

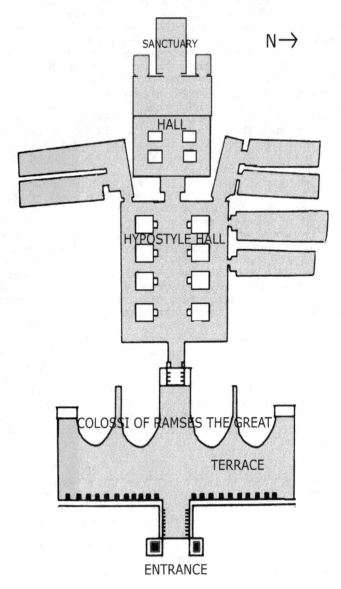

SANCTUARY

N→

HALL

HYPOSTYLE HALL

COLOSSI OF RAMSES THE GREAT

TERRACE

ENTRANCE

As little consolation, you can purchase a decent set of photographs (15 6x8) for 50LE. Abu Simbel is a phenomenal site and well worth the visit.

Nefertari Temple at Abu Simbel

Upon your return you may find that some of your fellow companions leave the ship at this stage and travel back to Luxor by coach as they have booked a week's holiday in a Luxor hotel (or maybe Aswan) and for them the cruise part of their holiday is over. You have to realise that the distance which has taken you three days to travel by boat, due to all the stop offs, will in fact only take the coach four hours back to Luxor.

If this happens the advantages are; more room at the tables, less people on the sundeck and less time waiting for your drinks! However there will probably be no entertainment on board that evening as numbers are small.

You could spend the rest of the day exploring on your own, choosing from some of the suggestions I've mentioned previously, or simply relax onboard.

If I was a first time traveller I would be inclined to do the former and make the most of the time left in Aswan, especially if you think the chances of you returning to Aswan are small.

An attractive small double sailed tourist boat with basic accommodation

DAY SIX:

All day is spent sailing leisurely back downstream to Luxor as the Nile's blue waters gently flow by. This gives you time to unwind and chill out by the pool and soak up the sun whilst assimilating the great amount of information you have been given by your tour guides. Or you can simply watch the world go by much as it did in ancient times, taking in the green palm lined banks, the children who play on the shores and wave endlessly at all the river-boats as they majestically sail past. The great river has sustained life in Egypt for the past 12,000 years and you can't help but marvel at its greatness as you cruise Pharaohs' Highway.

You will probably arrive back in Luxor early evening. Sometime during the day a departure meeting will be arranged where you will be given details about your pick up and flight times. You may also be asked to fill out a questionnaire asking you to rate your holiday and add any personal comments/complaints. I always fill this in truthfully highlighting bad practices, applauding good service and offering suggestions for improvement. For example last time I criticised the company's money-making visa trick, I suggested that tea-making facilities should be available in cabins and praised our female tour guide whom I thought was top-notch. Female tour guides are few and far between and really have to hold their own in a male dominated industry, often having to fend off jibes and snide comments from their male counterparts who obviously think it's no job for a woman.

100

In the evening there may be a farewell gathering arranged by your travel rep with cake served at the bar. The journey from Aswan back to Luxor, with no stops, will take approximately 12 hours.

DAY SEVEN:
Departure Day:
You will be served breakfast and an early lunch around 11.45am, before you leave.
If you are on full board you may be asked if you wish to keep your cabin until the last minute before departing for the airport. This usually involves an extra fee of around 150LE. If you don't wish to pay, you may have to vacate as early as 10am and use a communal cabin put aside for guests. Needless to say nearly everyone chooses to pay, either for ease or because they have a gippy tummy.
If you are on an all-inclusive holiday then this service should be free and you will be asked to leave your luggage outside your cabin for collection around 11.45am. All inclusive should continue up until the moment you leave, including free drinks. Vacation of your room is around 12.45 with a pick up time of 1pm.
By now your travel rep should have already advised you on the recommended amount of gratuities you should give the staff. Different companies have different systems but basically there are two types;
1. You pay just the staff you have come into contact, i.e. cleaners, waiters, reception, etc.
2. You pay a set amount to reception, which is then divided amongst all the boat staff.
The latter is becoming the more popular and at the time of writing this was £20 per person. You will probably be asked to put the money into a sealed envelope before handing it into reception. The staff will then ask for your cabin number in order to record who has paid. It will also be suggested that you give your Egyptian guide a personal tip of around £15 per person. So a couple will end up paying a total of £70 (700LE).
Even though I always paid the suggested amount to reception, I still find myself tipping those I have had personal contact with again privately. For example room cleaners, waiters, and baggage handlers who amaze me by carrying heavy suitcases, even two at a time, up very steep steps to the awaiting coach. Believe me that is no mean feat! I give the cleaner an extra 40LE, the waiter 20LE and the baggage hander 5LE. However, do not feel obliged to do this, as you have already paid and it is really down to how well you got on with the individuals concerned.

All these extra gratuities, which you are rarely told about when you book your holiday, can come to a considerable amount (not to mention a nasty surprise) and you will need to budget accordingly. You are never told that it is compulsory to provide these extra

101

monies, however their method of request does make it very hard to refuse, especially as you know the crew rely upon the extra gratuities to make up for their poor wages.

As you leave you may find some of the staff line up along the corridor in their best uniform, usually to the sound of a whistle. Whether you wish to give them an extra tip (which is basically what they are after) is entirely up to you.

Luxor Airport is fairly new and has become more like any modern airport with fixed price shops in contemporary style units, and an over-priced fast food restaurant and cafeteria.

You will have approximately an hour before your gate opens, which will give you just enough time to browse the shops and spend the last of your Egyptian notes on items you probably don't really need. ☺

TIP: Don't rush when your gate opens. Instead sit close by so you can keep an eye on how the queue is progressing. It will save you having to stand for 30 minutes, especially as all there is on the other side, is more uncomfortable seating, toilets and a small kiosk where you can buy a sandwich, biscuits, crisp etc. So you only end up waiting again, with even less to do.

TIP: If you see something you like at the airport but you can't afford it, you may like to try eBay on your return home. I particularly liked a set of leather pharaonic coasters priced £8 but they only had two sets left and I needed four. As luck would have it I managed to find the same set on eBay in the UK for £5 each, plus £2 postage, an overall saving of £10!

I must say I miss the old airport with its quirkiness and ramshackle appearance and I miss the numerous market style shops where you could still pick up a last minute bargain through bartering. Now the fixed prices are very similar to the UK and in some cases dearer. Oh well, I suppose that's the price of progress.

BOAT FACILITIES

All ships work on either a full-board or all-inclusive basis. You will probably find that your travel company usually has a fleet of boats of varying standards.

FULL-BOARD or ALL-INCLUSIVE
Full-board: Includes all your meals and drinks served at these times. What it does not include is the drinks you have around the pool, in your cabin, at the bar, or any bottled water. I have included a list of drink prices below so you can roughly work out what you think you will spend on drinks for the week per person if on 'full board'. Remember you will need to add bottled water to your requirements. Whatever you equate it to; I would suggest you add another third onto your estimate. People don't realise just how hot it can be in Egypt and how much liquid you need to consume to stop you becoming dehydrated. From experience I know 'full board' ship bars empty quite early on in the evening as people find the cost of drinks too expensive and retire to their cabins. Whereas 'all-inclusive' boats nightlife is far more sociable and usually lasts until midnight when the free bar closes.
All-inclusive: Should mean exactly that, i.e. free food and unlimited drinks (including bottled water) usually between the hours of 7am and 12pm (midnight). However not all types of drinks are free, just your basic ones, such as coffee and tea, local wine, beer, several soft drinks and bottled water. Imported drinks are not included. Drinks are served in the bar, restaurant and sundeck. They do not give you the bottle, but pour the drinks into small glasses - do not expect pints of beer. This means you constantly have to ask for refills or walk to the bar to get another.
TIP: If you strike up a good rapport with the waiter you may be able to get him to occasionally leave you the bottle. You can also ask for two drinks at a time, which may or may not be given.
TIP: if you're all-inclusive there will probably be no tea making facilities in your cabin, whereas there possibly will be on full board. (Swings and roundabouts I'm afraid) As I personally prefer all-inclusive I take a small low-power travel kettle, sachets of coffee and a packet of biscuits for cabin use, which I keep in my suitcase during the day.
TIP: If you are on an early excursion remember to get your bottled water the night before and store it in the mini bar to keep it cool.

Summary: The cost of drinks onboard ship is not cheap for example a bottle of beer (pint size) will set you back 50LE (£6.25) So you may want to consider all-inclusive in preference to full board. Normally if you were staying at a hotel I would recommend only booking bed and breakfast so you would be free to go out and about, but because you're on a cruise and confined to the boat for most of the time I would definitely go with all-inclusive. The drinks supplied in the cabin's refrigerated mini-bar are not free on either basis. Neither is room service. One small point, I have noticed that 'All-inclusive' waiters work at a much slower rate than 'Full board' waiters – strange that!

Remember to check when booking exactly what is included and excluded on either basis. The list below will give you an idea of the costs involved.

AVERAGE COST OF DRINKS ONBOARD

Bottle of Champagne	1900 LE
Bottle of wine	140 LE
Glass of wine	40 LE
Local small spirits (vodka, rum, whiskey, brandy)	35 LE
Imported spirits (small)	55 LE
Lagers and Beers (pint)	50 LE
Milkshakes	25 LE
Soft canned drinks (Pepsi, 7UP, Coke, Tonic etc)	14 LE
Fresh juice	20 LE
Canned juice	13 LE
Nescafe and Tea	14 LE
Espresso, Cappuccino, Latte	17 LE
Irish coffee	38 LE
Cocktails	40 LE
2 litre bottle of water (for your trips and cabin use)	15 LE
2 litre bottle of Coke/Pepsi	45 LE

*Prices are subject to change. Always check locally

So for example, if you have three bottles of lager and your partner three glasses of wine plus two bottles of water during a 24 hour period, the cost would be approximately 300LE per day. Times this by seven for the week and it comes to around 2100LE for the two of you, which is approximate £225. Of course on all-inclusive you wouldn't be restricted to the above amounts.

Any drinks bills, whether on full board or all-inclusive, can be settled at the time of purchase, or at the end of the week. I would recommend the former in order to help you budget. (Don't want a nasty surprise at the end of your holiday) As Egypt is mainly a Muslim country bare in mind that beer is very expensive and in many ways you are a captive audience!

Whilst on the boat you may come across some dodgy bartenders who, instead of signing and providing you with a drinks slip each time they serve you, instead provide you with free drinks. This has nothing to do with benevolence, as they expect you to give them money at the end of the cruise in return for their 'generosity'. That way the money goes directly into their pocket. They don't do it with everyone, but tend to target a few couples and give them the old tale of having too many wives and children to support. Whether you take them up on this 'offer' is entirely up to you.

LAYOUT

A typical sized boat will have approximately 50-55 cabins with a couple of larger suites. An average ship has five decks. Total guests aboard will be around 120 persons. An average ship size is 72m long x 14m wide x 11.5m high. Facilities can vary from boat to boat so ensure you ask at the time of booking. Also ask to look at a plan of the ship before you book.

RECEPTION

The reception area is where you book in, report any problems, hand your key in, pay your final bill, collect your passport etc. Some boats provide refreshing drinks and cool towels in this area on return from an excursion. There will be areas of seating where you can relax and talk, plus a section where the itinerary for the day will be posted including trips, meal times and evening entertainment.

LOUNGE BAR AND DISCO

The lounge bar is the perfect place to relax on comfortable sofas and enjoy a drink before dinner. It is also the area, where the evening entertainment takes place, which can be anything from a disco to a belly dancing night.

CABINS

Specific decks can usually be requested on booking, but are always subject to availability. Generally speaking the higher deck cabins have slightly better views, as they are well elevated above the waterline. Windows on lower decks are unlikely to open due to their closeness to the water. Also the lower deck cabins can smell strongly of diesel, as they are closer to the engine. However the air conditioning usually defeats this - as long as you do not turn it off! If you have any medical problem that affect your lungs, such as asthma, then I would suggest you mention this when booking and ask they reserve you a cabin away from the engines – i.e. front of boat and highest level. The noise and vibration of the engine is also worst on the lower level and can keep you awake. So, if at all possible avoid. However if you've booked late you may not have a choice. (We did it once and survived.☺)

Accommodation varies tremendously from ship to ship but usually each modest, but pleasant cabin consists of two single or double bed, en-suite bathroom/shower, wardrobe, writing desk, table and chairs, satellite TV, luggage stand, mini bar and air conditioning. They are modest but comfortable. The bathroom may contain either, a bath with overhead shower, or just a separate shower cubicle, washbasin, WC, bidet, waste-bin, hairdryer, electric socket, basic toiletries and towels. Again you may be able to stipulate either a twin or double bed when booking.

You will find extra bed covers are provided which you may be grateful for as the air-conditioning can make it feel pretty cool during the night. Of course you could turn it off, but depending on the month you are travelling, it could get hot really quickly.

Television programmes are pretty basic and come in many different languages, English, French, German, and Arabic. Probably the best you will get is a US News channel such as CNN or NBC and a half-decent film channel.

TIP: For this reason I pack a portable DVD player and a selection of films. Buying a wallet that holds several DVDs is better than taking separately boxed DVDs that bulk up your suitcase.

TIP: I also take an extension lead so I can place the DVD player close by. (I recommend you put the extension lead in a suitcase for safe keeping when you're not in the cabin)

The electricity supply onboard ship is 220 volts, 50 cycles, which means an adaptor is necessary (two-pronged) so remember to pack one. If you forget most gift shops in Egypt sell them – ask at reception.

The cabin will have a telephone but I always carry my mobile as texting is the cheaper option to keep in contact with family and friends, especially to let them know you've arrived safely.

TIP: Make sure you have international calling enabled on your mobile before leaving and if it's a 'pay as you go' phone, enough credit as all calls, whether outgoing or incoming, will be charged to your phone.

You will probably find a notice in the bathroom about not putting paper down the toilet. If this is this case a bin will be provided for the soiled toilet paper which is emptied daily. I know that old habits die hard and it is very easy to forget. If it does happen, don't worry as I've noticed over the years how much thinner and soluble the toilet paper has become, virtually breaking up as it hits the water. In the old days blocked toilets were a real problem, but not as much today. Your rep should be able to advise you on the situation.

Most cruise boats have safety deposit boxes available at no extra charge. They are usually located in your wardrobe and have an electronic combination lock which you set on arrival. The safe is usually big enough to hold your money, mobiles, jewellery, cards, passports, a camera and small camcorder.

TIP: Other valuables that won't fit in the safe I keep in a permanently locked suitcase. (E.g. DVD player, travel kettle, medicines)

Rooms are cleaned daily by the young men employees, and in my experience, very well.

You may find that your cabin staff are quite artistic and will leave you little surprises each day such as a pretty swan, crocodile, camel, boat and others, made from the towels left in your room. Their English is usually not that good, but enough to get by. With one of their favourite saying being, 'Ok, no problem,' which, after a while, isn't as reassuring as it was the first time you heard it. ☺

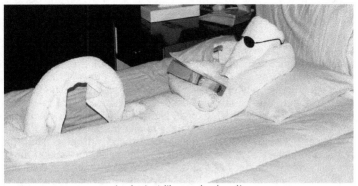
Looks just like my husband!

A room with a view. Even better a window that opens!

I like to stay on ships that have either a cabin balcony or a sliding patio-style window so I can lean out and watch the world go by and feel the breeze on my face as we sail. If possible avoid ships that have only fixed or half-sliding windows that restrict your ability to see out. Another reason for having a fully opening window is when I get back to our cabin I often open the window and leave the air-conditioning on. That way I get the best of both worlds, the warmth from outside and the refreshing coolness of the cabin. I admit, not very economical energy wise, but who cares, you're on holiday, enjoy yourself. Besides you've already paid the bill!

I recommend keeping your window closed when the ship is docked as the smell of diesel could get quite overpowering.

STAFF
Cruise ships have an all male Egyptian crew, with the only exceptions being female travel representatives. Different staff wear different uniforms, for example reception, administration and management are white collar, security and bar staff blue shirts, cabin cleaners grey uniform, ship maintenance workers green uniform, sailors navy blue uniform, kitchen staff black, or black and white check, and the captain a galabeya and turban.

The lower deck workers are usually not allowed in the tourist areas of the ship unless they are delivering supplies etc and spend most of their time at the back of the boat where all the noise and fumes from the engine accumulate. I asked the average life expectancy of these workers and was told it fell well below the national average of 70 years. I'm not surprised!

RESTAURANT
All meals are served in the restaurant. You should find international European-style and Egyptian cuisine widely available. Authentic dishes prepared for tourists are likely to be less spicy than the equivalent purchased in a local restaurant.

On your first visit to the ship's restaurant you will be asked your cabin number and shown to a table. This will be your table for the duration of your cruise. The tables usually seat 6 to 8 people who will remain your dining companions for the week. How much contact you have with them is entirely up to you but usually you are strangers at the beginning and friends by the end. You may also find that you are placed in the same group for all excursions so you are constantly in the same company for most of the day. And the same goes for the evening as people tend to socialise with those they have got to know around the table. Some people may find this a problem as they prefer to keep themselves to themselves, but folk aren't stupid and generally cotton on quickly and leave them alone. Honeymooners have a tendency to fall into this category. ☺

Mealtimes vary due to excursions but roughly speaking the times are;

- Breakfast   7.30 - 9.00am
- Lunch   12.30 - 2.00pm
- Afternoon tea   4,00 - 4.30pm
- Dinner   7.30 - 9.00pm.

Breakfast is buffet style with a choice of fruit juices, tea and coffee, cereal, rolls and breads, toast, cheese and meats, pastries, boiled eggs or omelette cooked to order. The wide choice means that vegetarians need not worry, as there are many suitable dishes available. You can eat as much as you like.

Lunch again is self-service, with a wide selection of salad starters, delicious soups with fresh rolls and bread. Main meals include, chicken, beef and fish dishes, fresh vegetables, pasta and rice. Desserts are numerous and you can often take your pick from superb pastries, sponges, or gateau. Fresh fruit is also widely available and can include oranges, bananas, melon and fresh dates.

Dinner is very similar to lunch, however for one night only you will enjoy a candle-lit meal that is completely table service, having chosen from a menu the day before.

On many cruises afternoon tea is when beverages, cakes and freshly cooked crepes or delicious pancakes are served, either on deck or in the bar.

Below are a few local Egyptian dishes you may come across;

- Tahini: Sesame seed paste, mixed with garlic, spices and some olive oil, and served as a dip with bread.
- Baba Ghannough: A dip made from tahini and mashed aubergines.
- Falafel (also known as ta'amia): Made from chickpeas pureed with garlic, fava beans, onions, egg and spices. A snack which is freshly cooked and stuffed into pita bread with tomatoes, lettuce and sauce.
- Stuffed vine leaves: Minced meat and rice wrapped in vine leaves.

If you're all-inclusive, meals are accompanied by a range of drinks, beer, coffee, wine, soft drinks, fruit juices, or just plain bottled water. Full-board usually has only tea, coffee, fruit juice concentrate and water available without payment. As a Muslim country the production of alcohol is restricted and the choice of beer is somewhat limited. The local beer (lager) is quite good, but not cheap if you're on full-board. There are imported beers available such as Heineken but these are even more expensive. Coffee is nearly always Nescafe. Some ships have coffee machines so it is possible to order cappuccino, espressos, etc. A variety of spirits and wines are readily available, though once again, expensive. The quality of local wines is improving but may not yet be up to the standards you are familiar with in the UK or the US. Karkade is a local drink made from hibiscus petals; it's a rich burgundy colour and very thirst-quenching. It can be served either hot or cold. If it's not already sweet enough try mixing it with fizzy lemonade for a delicious long, cool drink. Freshly squeezed juices such as orange and mango are widely available, with the local speciality being sugar cane juice.

If you are celebrating a special occasion, such as your wedding anniversary or birthday and would like to commemorate it with your travelling companions then let your travel rep know and they will arrange a treat for you. If, like myself, you're of a reserved nature then best to keep mum!

SHOPS

There will be a few shops onboard selling clothes, gifts, jewellery and souvenirs. Gold is always a popular purchase; especially the cartouche necklaces, on which you can have your name hieroglyphically inscribed. Compared to UK prices the cost of gold is good. TIP: Be sure to order a personal cartouche well in advance as orders can take a few days to make up.

A popular purchase in clothing is the traditional cotton robe known as a galabeya which is usually bought for the Egyptian Evening when guests dress up for fun and games. On board ship you will pay around 150-200LE for a basic costume. The galabeya is still the preferred dress of the countryside but due to western influences Egypt has witnessed its decline over the past 30 years, along with the traditional tarboosh or fez. This is particularly so in Northern Egypt in cities such as in Cairo and Alexandria.

Another favourite purchase is a tee-shirt with your name printed in hieroglyphs. In my experience they make novelty gifts for back home, but the quality is not very good and they tend to easily stretch out of shape, so I would only gently hand-wash them and preferably dry flat.

Gifts and souvenirs are numerous and vary in price tremendously. Toys, statues, mats, glassware, brassware, stoneware, alabaster, plates, ornaments.... the list is endless.

TIP: If you purchase any clothing, smell the garment first as most Egyptians are dedicated chain smokers and the smell of stale smoke can permeate the material making it difficult to get out.

TIP: You could purchase these items cheaper at any of the markets and shops around the ancient sites, but you have to be prepared to haggle. However be careful if you purchase gold as there are many con-men out there. The jewellery shop on the boat should give you a certificate that guarantees the gold's quality - ask before you buy. A couple of galabeyas from any of the markets should set you back around 80LE. I have even been offered them for 5LE each at the stalls near Philae.

Please be aware there are no government shops, even though some have this printed on their shop signs or windows. This is only to entice you in and make you think they are legitimate. Some jewellers who use this tactic have been known to sell tourists 9crt gold at 18crt prices.

As the years have gone by I have seen Egyptian prices steadily creep up, so much so, that the chances of you getting a 'really good bargain' today have been greatly reduced, but there are still some to be had if you're willing to do the haggling.

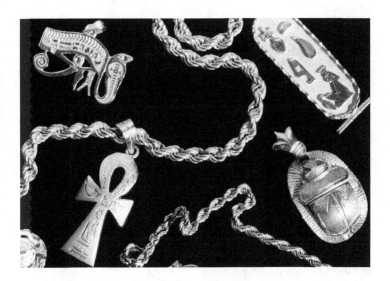

The photo shows some of the more popular ancient Egyptian designs namely; Eye of Horus (top left), Cartouche (top right), Ankh (bottom left), Scarab (bottom right).

Prices will vary as to where you buy your souvenirs. Below is a list of the cheapest to the dearest;

- Street sellers with no stalls
- Market traders
- Local village shops
- Ancient Site sellers
- Ship and hotel shops
- Duty Free at Airport

SUNDECK

On the sundeck you can sunbathe, take a dip in the pool, photograph the scenery, or just chill out under a sunshade with a book and cold drink. Other popular amenities could include Jacuzzi, fitness equipment, hammocks, swings and table tennis. The pools onboard Nile cruise ships are not swimming pools but dip pools, so don't expect to be able to take a daily swim! You may find parasols in short supply so grab one at the start of your sunbathing session, otherwise when you've had enough sun, you may not be able to find one.

Be aware if you are sunbathing at the front of the boat near the steps to the pilot's area, you may be asked to join him by one of the boat's 'lower deck' crew. These are the manual workers; usually dressed in green overalls, as opposed to the white shirt and black trousers worn by the waiters, guides, shop keepers etc. These manual workers are not normally seen in the tourist areas of the boat, but if you are close enough they may beckon you to come and join them. Choosing whether to go or not is entirely up to you, but if you are a woman I would suggest that you do not go alone. Not that you are in any particular danger, but you will feel more comfortable with a friend around. They will probably ask if you want to toot the horn, or hold the steering wheel (whilst sat on the pilot's knee if he can get away with it) and may suggest you have your photograph taken with the pilot. As you may have guessed, their ulterior motive is money as they will expect a tip for having 'shown you around'. So, if you don't want to be bothered, just shake you head and indicate you are not interested with a dismissive wave of the hand.

Occasionally the wind at the back of the sundeck swirls around and if you are not careful belongings can be snatched away overboard - e.g. sunhats, magazines, etc. However all is not necessarily lost, as you may be surprised when you look overboard and find one of the manual crew below has your lost item in their hand. This is because the bottom deck acts like a funnel and drags most things back towards the boat where they are working. It is normal practice to thank the men with a suitable tip - after all they have rescued your precious belongings.

ON-BOARD EVENING ENTERTAINMENT

Local Nubian dancers entertaining in the Lounge bar

Your tour company will have planned your evening entertainment for the week which could be anything from Nubian dancers, Whirling Dervish, a local band or belly dancing. And yes, the belly dancer will ask for volunteers! The entertainment takes place in the lounge bar and starts around 8pm. Once during your cruise you will be invited to an 'Egyptian Evening' where you will be expected to dress up like a local and get involved in fun and party games, which can include a treasure hunt, a competition to find the best mummy wrapper and a contest to find the best 'Walk like an Egyptian' dancer. A photograph and video may be taken during the Egyptian Evening which you can purchase on DVD.

112

Generally speaking there is no pressure to join in and if you prefer you can always retire to the sundeck with your drinks for a bit of peace and quiet and just listen to the waters of the Nile drift slowly by.

OTHER COMMON FACILITIES
Other free facilities may include disco room, library, music system in cabin, gaming facilities such as, backgammon or chess, jogging track and free wake-up calls.

Other chargeable facilities may include; internet, massage, pool table, boat doctor, laundry service, files transfer onto DVD (e.g. photos from camera) hairdresser, beautician and fitness centre.

Regarding the internet, I know many of the newer ships do provide wireless internet connection, for example the new Sonesta Nile cruisers, but not many of the older ships do. However internet connection is usually available around the reception area and is chargeable by the half hour. A common price is 40LE for 30 minutes.

Typical pool area. Size is usually around 15 to 20 feet

GENERAL INFORMATION

RESEARCH
Probably one of the best pieces of advice I can give you is to ensure you purchase a good Egyptian travel guide and read up on the sites as this will breathe life into any organised tours, adding interest, understanding and wonderment.

Without a basic knowledge of Egypt's illustrious and glorious past, there is a danger you'll simply become bored as you visit one ruin after another. This particularly applies if only one of you has a fascination with the ancient civilisation and the other person is merely tagging along for their partner's sake.

I would also suggest you make a list of specific points of interests you would like to see or photograph at each location. Not only will it give you a sense of satisfaction and your visit purpose, but imagine how impressed your companion(s) will be by your knowledge, especially if you can also answer the inevitable questions posed by your tour guide during every visit.

I recommend you pack at least one book which you can refer to on a daily basis in order to refresh your insight for the following day's excursions. (Naturally, I would suggest this one.☺)

BOOKING
There are usually some very reasonably priced late-deals, which is great if you don't have to book your holiday too far in advance but ensure you know the operating company, or you are able to check their credibility. To fully enjoy your Egyptian cruise, it's important to choose an experienced company who operate some of the three hundred plus boats that sail between Luxor and Aswan. As well as your local travel agency there are many online sites that can help you make an informed decision.

TEMPERATURE
For most westerners who prefer a more temperate climate November March and April, are usually good choices. December, January and February are also okay, but these are Egypt's winter months and as such can be a little on the cool side. On the other hand Egyptian summers are scorching which means fewer crowds and cheaper prices. Basically it depends on whether you can tolerate high temperatures. As a rough guide the chart below demonstrates the average monthly temperature.

JAN	FEB	MAR	APR	MAY	JUN	JUL	AUG	SEP	OCT	NOV	DEC
64F	65F	70F	72F	104F	110F	113F	110F	106F	100F	72F	69F

There is usually a breeze coming off the Nile which helps to make the heat a little more bearable. The further south you travel the hotter it becomes. So Aswan can be several degrees hotter than Luxor and Cairo several degrees cooler. Depending on the time of year, when you first step off the boat in the mornings it can feel as if the heat is literally scorching your lungs. This is due to the huge difference between the air conditioned boat and the heat outside. It will wear off, as you gradually become acclimatised.

HEALTH AND SAFETY MATTERS

Many cruise ships do have English speaking doctors which they can call on 24 hours. Prices for doctors are difficult to give as each set their own fees, but expect to pay in the region of 200-300LE for a visit and around 30-40LE for a prescription.

Many UK prescription drugs are available over the counter in Egyptian pharmacies but they may be called by a different name and unless you know, it is best not to take any chances. So if you have prescribed medicines ensure that you take them with you.

Only use tap water for washing and showering. Egyptian water is highly chlorinated and not suitable for our western stomachs. Only drink bottled water, this includes cleaning your teeth. The recommended intake is 1-2 litre per person per day. You will be told that ice cubes provided by the ship are made from bottled mineral water and therefore safe. Personally I don't take the chance and never have them in my drinks.

Turn off your air conditioning for 10 minutes when you return from the sundeck as this will help you acclimatise from the baking heat to the coolness of your cabin. This also applies when you return from any trips.

It can get very dark in your cabin at night so I recommend you leave the bathroom light on with the door slightly ajar, so if you do have to get up to go to the toilet you won't fall over anything.

Take a pocket torch in case of power cuts.

Besides food poisoning, other causes of stomach upsets can be; change of diet, sunstroke, dehydration, alcohol over-indulgence. I would advise taking plenty of anti-diarrhoea medication with you (e.g. Imodium), also painkillers that are gentle on the stomach, (e.g. Paracetamol) and a stomach remedy (e.g. Gaviscon). However if you do forget, your travel representative or a local chemist should be able to help.

You may find that some Egyptian bugs do not respond to European anti-diarrhoea tablets and you will need to purchase local medicines. Again your travel rep or reception will be able to help you.

Because I suffer with a bad neck I always pack my own pillow. I simply use it at night then store it away in a suitcase during the day. This ensures it isn't taken away by accident when the cabin crew clean the room. Most beds I can usually deal with ok, but not having the correct type of pillow can ruin my holiday. If you suffer similarly you may want to consider doing the same.

When first dining you are advised to take only one type of salad dish until your stomach adjusts to the different herbs, spices and oils used in Egyptian cuisine.

Do not be tempted to swim in the Nile or canals as you are at GREAT risk of exposure to bacterial infections, hepatitis, and parasites.

Dead camel floating in the Nile

Also avoid walking barefoot for the same reasons as above, this includes inside the temples and pyramid sites. I often see 'Kemetics' (modern day followers of the Ancient Egyptian religion) meditating or wandering around the temples barefoot, especially Karnak, and I often wonder if they are aware of the risks.

Drink only bottled water: A two litre bottle bought off boat will cost anything between 5-9LE depending on your haggling skills.

It is important to remember to drink plenty of water while in Egypt even if you don't feel thirsty, this is particularly true during the summer months to prevent dehydration and stomach upsets. If you do start to feel ill with the heat you will be surprised just how quickly a drink of water can revive you. Remember water, sun-cream and sunhat! Don't leave without any of these. I have seen many a person collapse around the sites due to the overbearing heat. When this happens the person will be helped to a shady part of the site and told to rest and drink water. The vast majority recover quite quickly. If this happens to you get back to the air-conditioned coach as soon as possible and do not be tempted to carry on as it quite obvious that the heat is putting your body under too much strain.

TIP: I usually buy a couple of small bottle of water in the UK (ones will pull cap) and constantly fill them up to use each day. It's a more convenient size for storage, less weight and easier to drink from.

The water you are carrying will get quite warm, but there is not much you can do about that I'm afraid, unless you carry a flask which will add considerable weight to your pack. To be honest you can get that thirsty in the heat that you won't care what temperature the water is!

For the same reason don't stay too long on the sundeck. It's no use suffering from sunstroke which could ruin your holiday. I always stay under a parasol and I still come home brown. On the 7th October at 1pm it was 97.5F degrees on the sundeck and it hadn't reached its peak. Remember the heat is really intense in Egypt and you will burn very quickly. If you start feeling sickly or get a headache heed the message your body is telling you and get out of the sun. Obviously sickness can greatly affect your enjoyment and ability to go on organised tours.

Malaria tablets: At present these are deemed unnecessary, unless you intend travelling into the more remote areas of Egypt and in fact malaria tablets have many side effects including sickness and diarrhoea. However mosquito repellents are another matter and I would strongly advise you to pack these in order to minimize the chances of being bitten. The worst time for getting bitten is after dusk. Mosquito bites can be very irritating. If you are bitten use an appropriate antiseptic cream and try to avoid scratching the infected area as the lump will become itchier! I find gently stroking the lump with my fingertips or pressing just around the edges causes less irritation and helps to alleviate the overwhelming urge to scratch. A cold compress can also work wonders. As can calamine lotion. The lumps can last many days but you will be pleased to know that you are less likely to be bitten on a cruise as mosquitoes prefer stagnant water, to fast flowing rivers. The worst time for being bitten will be at the evening Sound and Light Shows at Karnak and Philae.

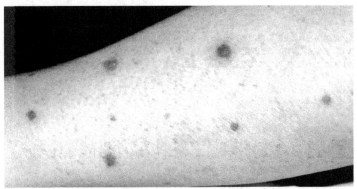

Lovely mosquito bites. I should have remembered the cream!

I always take back-up food with me whenever I travel to Egypt. The reasons being, because if I get any type of stomach upset I know once I am feeling better I won't want to chance the ship's food again, which probably caused my problem in the first place. With this in mind I take things such as Pot Noodles, cuppa soups, biscuits, coffee, chocolate, crisps and sweets – anything that doesn't take up too much space or weight in my suitcase.

TIP: To conserve space crush down the pot noodle contents and empty it into a plastic bag. Repeat for each pot noodle. Then take only two pot noodle cartons with you, stacked together and re-

117

stuffed with as many of the plastic bags as you can to protect the carton against splitting in transit. Wrap up the rest of the plastic bags and store in your suitcase. In Egypt reuse the same carton as much as possible, remembering to wash it out only with bottled water, not tap water.

You may find you suffer from swollen ankles whilst in Egypt. This is a common water retention problem and you will probably find they go down overnight with rest and the coolness of your cabin.

Most of Egyptian bottled water comes from wells and may contain a lot of dissolved salts. If possible check the labels and choose the one with least salts - this is usually a 'deep well' water source. Below are just a few of the different bottled water companies and their water content:

Mg/L	Siwa	Nestle	Delta
Calcium	5.0	16.0	30.0
Magnesium	6.0	6.0	13.44
Sodium	42.0	16.0	43.0
Potassium	16.0	1.0	3.6
Bicarbonate	110.0	88.0	200.08
Sulphate	14.0	17.0	14.5
Chloride	29.0	9.0	17.7
Silica	19.0	9.0	24.0
Total Dissolved Solids	200.0	132.0	262.0

As you can see Nestle has the least salt content, which seniors may find suits them better. Unfortunately you don't always get a choice, which means you just have to go with the flow. (Sorry for the pun)

MONEY MATTERS

If you are travelling to a UK airport by car, be sure to book your car parking space before as discounts are usually available for pre-booking, especially online.

Alternatively if you are travelling some distance consider booking into a hotel near the airport for the night before as many include free weekly parking in the price.

If you intend purchasing your holiday money before you travel, don't leave it until the last minute, shop around as you could make a considerable saving on the airport's bureau de change.

The local currency is the Egyptian pound.

At present the maximum amount of Egyptian currency that can be taken into Egypt is 5,000LE per person. However this is subject to change and you will be informed as to the current limit when you purchase your currency. There is no limit on the amount of foreign money you can take into the country, except you have to declare anything over 10,000 US$ per person, or its equivalent.

Notes are in denominations of 50 piastre, 5,10,20,50,100 200 & 500LE. Some of the notes look very similar on first glance, so when buying souvenirs be absolutely certain which note you are handing over – 50 piastres, not 50 Egyptian pounds! I am sure you will be told of your mistake if it's a 50 piastres note, but not if it's 50LE! That's equivalent to £5 GBP and a definite windfall for most Egyptians.

The average hourly rate for a waiter is 1LE.

The only coin you are likely to see is the 1LE which was introduced in 2006. If you get any, hold on to them for tipping.

I use only Egyptian currency and a credit card (if I'm pushed) whilst in Egypt.

I purchase my Egyptian notes on arrival at the airport as the exchange rate is better than the UK. (Ask that they include some small notes and 1LE coins)

Debit and Credit cards such as American Express, Diners Club, MasterCard and Visa are all widely accepted but outside of the big cities their usage is extremely limited as Egypt is still largely a cash-based country. There are cash machines in the main towns. Hotels and ships will accept major cards. Credit and debit card usage does however come with many charges such as;

- Foreign exchange 'load' fee of up to 2.75% of the sum spent.
- Interest charges from the moment cash is withdrawn, often at rates of up to 30% APR, even if you have no outstanding balance.
- A cash withdrawal fee of around 2.5% (or £3) when you take money out of an ATM using your credit card.

You can find out the best cards to use abroad by checking money consumer websites online. The upside of using your credit card to pay for certain goods and services relating to your holiday, as opposed to your debit card, is that you get extra protection under Section 75 of the UK Consumer Credit Act. (Read before you travel).

Traveller's cheques are accepted in the main towns but it's getting harder and harder to find places that accept them, although you should have no problem on the ship. To avoid additional exchange rate charges, travellers are advised to take travellers cheques in US Dollars, Euros or Pounds Sterling.

Scottish and Northern Ireland bank notes are not accepted for exchange in Egypt.

Banks will charge a commission fee to change your currency or travellers cheques and will require you to present your passport. An official receipt will be given when exchanging money, which should be kept for inspection. Banking hours are normally Sun-Thurs 0830-1400. Whilst in Luxor a representative from the local bank may visit the boat or they may have facilities at reception. The daily exchange rate is fixed by the government so it should be the same at any bank, hotel or ship. Your Travel Rep should advise you during your welcome meeting.

Avoid paying for anything in sterling (or your own currency) for example at restaurants and shops as they do what is known as a

'Dynamic Currency Conversion' which is not a set exchange rate and is always unfavourable to the customer, which means you end up paying far more than you would have done had you used local currency. (This applies to all destinations, not just Egypt.)

Tipping, or baksheesh as it is called in Egypt, is a way of life and porters, site attendants, waiters etc will all expect a small tip for their services. The average is 1-2LE for a porter and 2-3LE for a coach driver, bartender and bell captain. Be sure to hold on to any small notes and coins, which are particularly useful for tipping and for buying cheaper items. Change always seems to be in short supply in Egypt, even the locals do not like to part with small notes! Tipping is very important as it can make up as much as 50% of their weekly wage. However, on a Nile cruise, you may be asked to pay a lump sum at the end which covers all tipping. The word baksheesh and the idea of tipping was introduced by soldiers when Egypt was a British colony. When they gave the children money they would call it baksheesh, which is an Indian word for 'free money'. The Egyptians then developed it to mean 'tipping after a service was offered'. (So we have no one but ourselves to blame)

If you end up with some of the small notes and coins left over at the end of your holiday, you will probably find when you arrive at the airport that some of the local baggage carriers are eager to exchange them for English coins, which they have acquired from tourists who have just arrived. This is an ideal way of getting rid of them as fair exchange is no robbery, and everyone is happy.

OPTIONS FOR GETTING AROUND LUXOR:

Walk: You could walk into town but this will depend on how far your ship is moored from the centre, how hot it is, and if you feel up to running the gauntlet of the locals who are always on the lookout for unsuspecting tourists. Shopkeepers, taxi and calashe drivers, felucca and motorboat operators, restaurant owners, children, market traders...... the list is endless. My advice is, just keep walking with determination, purpose and a dismissive hand gesture to anybody that tries to block your way.

Taxi: This is probably the best option if you know where you want to go, for example a specific hotel or venue. There are hundreds of blue and white taxis on every street corner of Luxor so you will never have a problem finding one. On the contrary your problem will be fending off the dozens of cab drivers that will swamp you as soon as you leave the boat. Don't be afraid to play them off against each other in order to get the best price and be prepared for some animated scenes as they all vie for your custom.

Caleshe: (Horse and carriage) Most likely your tour guide will advise against the traditional caleshe for safety reasons and if you do get a skittish horse, it can be quite hair-rising. I remember once telling a particularly persistent caleshe driver that I wanted to walk, as it was healthier for me. But his quick retort was - it wasn't healthy for him! My advice is try not to get too uptight with regards to the hassle, I'm afraid it comes with the territory. Having said that, Caleshe drivers are notoriously aggressive and rude, especially towards women, and even I have been known to lose my rag with them on occasion. A caleshe driver will say 'small price' but then at the end of the journey they will charge you for his horse, saying 'he is cheap, but his horse isn't. Always, always agree a price in Egyptian pounds before getting into the carriage, make sure he understands it's for a return trip (if that's what you want) and do not give him any money until the end of the trip.

PHOTOGRAPHY

Photography is strictly forbidden at military installations, public works and government buildings. Tourists should not take photographs that include official uniformed personnel.

Always ask permission before photographing local Egyptians, and expect to be asked for a tip in return. Around the sites you will often be approached by local men or boys who will indicate that you should photograph them. Again if you do, they will expect a tip. I always let them know before I take a picture, how much I am willing to pay, 1LE, but remember that will 'buy' you one picture only. If you take more, they will expect more. Plus, even if you only take one they will still try it on and ask for another pound for his horse, camel, ailing mother etc. Be firm and say, no. (La)

Most ships nowadays provide a DVD copying service, so if you do run out of space on your memory cards you can have your images transferred onto DVD/CD - freeing up space again.

If you are still using a film camera take plenty of film with you as the chances of you finding any are very limited. Plus you never know the conditions under which the film has been stored.

Don't worry about x-ray machines ruining your photography. All my cameras, digital storage devices and films have been through the airport equipment many times and I've never lost a single photo.

Below are some photographic tips and suggestions:
1. Make sure you take plenty of memory cards with you for your camera and don't be afraid to snap away because the beauty of digital is that you can easily review and delete any photos that don't come up to scratch.
2. If you don't have a SLR camera with interchangeable lens then if possible take a camera that has a decent zoom and wide angle range.
3. If there are two of you, take more than one camera.
4. Remember to photograph the approach to Philae from the boat.
5. Views from a felucca can make for lovely pictures especially around the Aswan area.
6. Remember to photograph your ship; maybe from a felucca.

7. Don't forget your camera on the balloon trip and make sure you secure it to your wrist via the camera strap as you don't want to accidently drop it over the side!
8. If you can't fit your camera in the cabin safe, put it in a locked suitcase.
9. Every time you visit a new site, immediately photograph your ticket so you can identify which photographs relate to which site when you get home.
10. Couples: Ask a fellow traveller to photograph the two of you together at least once at every site. (It's easily forgotten as you are ushered around.)
11. Although you can't photograph the inside of tombs anymore there are still places where you can get some good examples of original ancient colours. These include Kom Ombo, Karnak and Deir El Bahri. (Our website includes many examples of these)

CLOTHING AND ACCESSORIES

It can be hot throughout the year in Egypt; especially during the day so loose fitting 100% light cotton clothing is the most comfortable and most sensible choice as it allows your skin to breathe in the hot weather.

Take a good pair of sunglasses, comfortable walking shoes (or trainers), plenty of sun cream and a good sunhat.

Women in particularly are best advised to dress conservatively. It is wise not to have bare shoulders or wear revealing tops or shorts in towns and villages and especially when visiting mosques and churches as you could risk causing offence. Egypt is a mainly Muslim country and Egyptians, particularly the older generation, do not appreciate seeing flesh on show. Likewise, women showing too much skin can also provoke unwanted attention from the younger Arab men. This is particularly true with regards to skimpily clad young women. It is not my intention to be moralistic here, this information is provided because I wish to tell you how it is, and not what you, or I, think it should be like. Around the main sites, hotels and on board ship this is not a problem as they are used to women in western-style dress.

It is also not acceptable for men to go bare-chested except by the pool and women going topless is not allowed anywhere.

Jacket and tie or cocktail dresses are not necessary as evenings are informal. Casual dress is okay but I usually take a couple of dresses that could be classed as 'smart evening wear'. Plus, it's nice sometimes just to spend an hour or two getting yourself ready for the evening as it makes you feel as if you are on holiday.

The months in Egypt follow the same seasonal pattern as the UK, e.g. July is summer and January is winter but obviously Egypt's are a lot hotter and milder respectively, especially the further south you travel. As most of us choose to visit during the cooler seasons I would suggest you take some warmer items of clothing just in case the temperatures drop, especially in the evening. E.g. one light cardigan or jumper, trousers, light jacket etc. You can see a real-time temperatures page for most of the major Egyptian cities on our website which I suggest you check out regularly during the few weeks before you travel to see exactly what the weather is like.

FACTS AND CUSTOMS
Ninety-six percent of Egypt is desert.

The population of Egypt totals 82 million, which puts a huge burden on the country's resources.

The language is Egyptian Arabic; however English is widely spoken in the tourist areas.

Religion: 75% of the population are Muslim and 25% Christian.

Egypt was a strong Christian country between the years 300-700 AD and is considered to be the birthplace of monasticism. Monasticism began as a life of complete solitude and contemplation with individuals living alone in caves and other small dwellings. Later monasteries were formed in Egypt at the end of the third century, making Egyptian monasteries the oldest in the world. The father of monasticism is considered to be St. Anthony the Great a Copt from Upper Egypt who lived 105 years from A.D. 251 until 356. He is accredited with establishing the basics of living the life of a monk.

Muslims pray five times a day at dawn, mid-day, late-afternoon, sunset, late evening and follow the teachings of the Prophet Mohammed. The month of Ramadan is a time when Muslims fast from dawn until sundown, abstaining from food, drink, and sexual relations with their spouses. Muslims follow five pillars, each of which gets them closer to paradise. The pillars are; faith, fasting, prayer, charity and a pilgrimage to Mecca at least once in their lifetime.

Muslims are allowed five wives, but wives only one husband.

Quite often you will see Egyptian male friends greeting each other with a hug and kiss on both cheeks, but not friends of the opposite sex. You may also see, as you walk around the towns that many boys will hold hands. This is common practice.

As a foreigner when you are saying goodbye to a member of the opposite sex do not kiss them on the cheek, but stick to a hand shake.

Showing open affection to your own partner in public places is definitely frowned upon.

There is a definite class system in Egypt so don't be surprised if you see one man chastising another quite severely. I once witnessed a hotel manager slapping a poor pool attendant a number of times around the head. The 'lower class' must show respect and will bow to their 'superiors' at all times. Again, whether you agree, or not, this is the way of things in Egypt. As much as you may want to say something I would suggest you don't because once you take your leave you could cause the person even more trouble.

Black is the preferred colour for Egyptian woman as it is the colour of respect.

There are two types of education in Egypt, government and private. Children attend nursery school from 4 years old. Private schools have to be paid for, but are very good and based on the British system, with all studies being taught in English. From secondary school you choose to go to either college or university. It takes a student of archaeology four years, plus three years of training to obtain a licence. All archaeologists are freelance.

Wages: 1500LE is an average monthly wage for an Egyptian. However a protest on the streets of Cairo in 2010 supported a national monthly minimum wage of 1200LE clearly demonstrated that the lower paid workers earn a lot less. Most tour guides from Cairo earn an average of 8000LE a month, working two weeks on, one week off.

There are approximately 75 staff on board the ship. Cleaners work one month on, one week off.

To get a good job you must speak at least two languages and have computer skills.

There is a high rate of unemployment in Egypt and according to the World Bank, nearly 44 percent of Egyptians are extremely poor (unable to meet minimum food needs), poor (unable to meet basic food needs), or near-poor (able to meet some basic food needs).

There is no pension scheme in Egypt, so Egyptians have to work long hours to save for their future. Tax is at 15%.

Military service is compulsory for men in Egypt. They serve one year if they have a good education. Two years if they have a poor education and three years if they have no education. However, if they are the only son, or their father has died, then they would not have to serve at all.

Women from the north of Egypt (e.g. Cairo) are more westernised, with less traditions and restrictions than women from the south (e.g. Luxor).

Northern women are more career-minded, whereas southern women tend not to work and the vast majority are not allowed to mix with tourists.

Unlike northern women who earn a wage, southern women prefer to buy gold and put it in safety boxes in their home, rather than bank it, as gold appreciates in value.

Ninety-five percent of people working in the tourist industry are men. Women do not have it easy and have to constantly prove themselves. Our last tour guide was a woman and without a shadow of a doubt she was the best we have encountered.

There are government hospitals that Egyptians pay insurance for, but most Egyptians prefer to use private hospitals as these are far better staffed and equipped.

In most cases an Egyptian man chooses his wife. It used to be the father but times have changed, especially in the north of the country.

Marriage is more expensive in the south as the husband-to-be is expected to buy a flat and gold presents for his future wife. A flat costs around 150,000LE

The average age to get married used to be 15 for females and 20 for males, however due to the rising cost of marriage this is now 30 for females and 40 for males.

Southern women are not allowed a relationship before marriage but in the north they are more relaxed and couples can live together and save in order to prepare for their marriage and family.

Bedouins are Arabic-speaking desert nomads. In Egypt there are two types of Bedouins, those living in the Western Desert who can be dangerous and those living in the Eastern Desert who are a kinder people and have embraced tourism. Bedouins hold a party during which time if a woman reveals her face to a single man she is inviting him to choose her as his bride. When the family get together if the girl is happy with her choice she puts sugar in her tea. If no sugar, then she does not want to marry him. However the final say is with her father. After the wedding they spend thirty days alone in a tent in the desert and then move back to live in his family's tent. To give birth, a Bedouin wife must go into the desert with two older women and just water and a knife, as men consider it impolite to hear her screams.

TRAVELLING ALONE

General travel throughout Egypt:

I am often asked if I would recommend travelling alone. This depends entirely upon the individual and how confident and comfortable you feel with the idea. If you have any doubts I would suggest travelling in a group. It will also depend upon your gender; women on their own are likely to feel far more uncomfortable and at risk than men. The UK Foreign Office advises that women take extra caution when travelling alone to Egypt. (See our 'Telling You How It Is' section) I would also recommend that people on their own do not travel into smaller towns, villages or rural areas unless they are with somebody they trust, who knows the area and language. This is especially true at night.

On a Cruise:

For the above reasons I firmly believe a Nile cruise is particularly good for lone travellers as they are in a relatively safe environment and have access to help and advice should you require it. Also meal times are usually spent with the same people, as are the organised tours. This allows you to meet and chat with others, (or not, as the mood takes) so generally speaking you should feel safer and less isolated than you may in hotel rooms. Personally, as a woman, I would be far happier travelling alone on a cruise.

125

GETTING MARRIED IN EGYPT

I have been asked on occasion whether it is possible to get married during a Nile Cruise and the answer I'm afraid is, no.

It is possible to get married in Egypt, but it is not easy and you certainly can't get married around the ancient sites.

In order to get married you have to meet certain government requirements and time periods (if divorced or widowed) before you can get wed. Plus, a marriage in Egypt is only legal if it is a civil ceremony performed at a local marriage court. There could also be some doubt as to whether the marriage would be classed as legal in your own country of origin. 'Orfi weddings' (secret marriages) are not legal.

MISCELLANEOUS

Packed lunches are provided if you are travelling on excursions during meal times, for example to Abu Simbel.

Egypt is not a particularly popular holiday destination for young children. By this I mean, most youngsters are not interested in visiting 'ruins' every day, plus many travel companies do not allow children under the age of twelve on cruises. Teenagers who have studied Ancient Egypt can usually appreciate the sites and have a great holiday. The average age of those taking cruises I would say is between 45 and 60. Children/teenagers are usually very thin on the ground. I would not recommend taking babies on a cruise.

Due to the building of the high dam there are no longer any crocodiles in the Nile between Cairo and Aswan.

The Nile cruise boats are flat-bottomed and as there is no tide, you will not get seasick.

Sunday is the first working day of the week.

Shops are generally open 10am to 9pm in winter and 9am to 10pm in summer. In the tourist areas some shops may stay open outside these hours. Do not be surprised if you are offered tea or a soft drink in larger shops, as this is customary.

Due to operational demands Nile Cruise itineraries can be subject to alteration at very short notice and during certain periods, you may find that the boat has to sail after dark, thereby reducing daylight sailing hours and scenic views.

There can be over 30,000 British tourists in Egypt in any given week during the main tourist season.

Over 12 million tourists visit Egypt every year.

The tourist trade accounts for over 10% of the country's annual revenue.

TELLING YOU HOW IT IS
What the brochures don't include:

Now for the promise which I gave at the beginning of this book, about telling you 'how it is' and not just offering you the romantic side of a Nile cruise. This was my main motivation for writing this book when, after visiting Egypt for the first time in the early 1990s, I was both shocked and annoyed by some of the things that happened which we were never advised about. In my experience there are three main reasons why most people don't choose to go, or return, to Egypt. These are hassle, illness and terrorism.

HASSLE IN EGYPT
This can come in many forms such as; pestering, tipping, haggling, scams, con-artists and intimidation (thankfully, not very common).

Pestering: In Egypt pestering can prove to be somewhat overwhelming, not to mention a little intimidating to the foreign traveller and admittedly it can seem as if there are no genuine people in Egypt. Obviously this is not the case, but unfortunately, as a tourist you rarely come into contact with the more sincere people, but are constantly subjected to the ones who are only after your money. Therefore the benefits of a Nile cruise have to be noted. Firstly, the boat helps to shield you against the constant pestering that people who are staying in hotels experience every time they walk out of the door. Also the majority of times you do venture off the boat you will be in the company of your fellow passengers and tour guide and unlikely to be pestered excessively.
Another advantage is your representative usually travels on the cruise so they are readily available in cases of emergencies or simple advice, including hassle problems.
Young men can be a particularly nuisance and are often intent on wearing down their victim until you buy something just to get rid of them. After visiting Kom Ombo temple I remember one young man trying to sell me a bracelet for 5LE as we made our way back to the ship. The bracelet looked as if it was ready to fall apart as he held it. I said a polite, 'no thanks', but he continued to pester, as I continued to say, no. By the time we had reached the boat he was offering me four bracelets for 5LE. It was at this point that I pointed out that the only bag I was carrying was a camera bag and I had no money with me. (This wasn't true, but I knew it would probably get him off my back.) The cheeky imp then immediately lost his false tourist smile and turned on me shouting angrily, 'What have you come to Egypt for, if you have no money to buy anything!' To which I replied, 'To see the temples and tombs and not to spend my hard-earned money buying rubbish souvenirs from pestering kids such as you.' He got the message and swiftly moved on. Whilst I don't advocate losing your temper, sometimes

127

you have to be quite firm with the male youths that work the tourist areas.

Tipping: Away from the boat you will be expected to tip every time you are offered a service, have a meal, drink, etc. Tipping can really mount up, so make sure you have budgeted for this extra expense you are rarely warned about, otherwise you could find yourself running short of money. If someone does something for you in the tourist areas they are usually after a tip, e.g. ancient sites, airport, hotel. Don't feel obliged to pay every time, but only if you feel they deserve it. You may have been advised by others who have travelled to Egypt to take things such as felt tip pens and sweets to give out as gifts to the local children. I did this the first time I visited Egypt but made the mistake of handing out a couple of pens in the centre of Luxor. The next minute I had children coming out of the woodwork until I was completely surrounded by tugging and snatching hands all fighting to get them off me.

In the end they were even fighting amongst themselves with more than a few turning on the tears and begging me to give them one. Their ages ranged from as little as four to fourteen, so you can imagine some of them were quite strong. I never thought I was in any danger but for a while it was decidedly uncomfortable. Eventually a passing man shouted something in Arabic and they let go and I was able to make my escape. Since that incident I only give out gifts in more controlled circumstances; maybe thrown from the boat, or where I know the numbers are small; for example at the ancient sites. The adults also like the pens, plus the toiletries such as shampoo and soap that are made available in your cabin. I suggest you remove the pens from their packaging and hand them out singly. Don't be surprised by what you may be asked for. My husband was once asked literally for the shirt off his back, whilst one woman asked me for my sandals and another my lipstick. Needless to say these requests were politely refused.

Haggling: In all bazaars and shops haggling is common practice and can be fun, if approached in the right frame of mind. Your guide will be able to give you information on the best way to haggle and also provide guidance on what you should expect to pay for common souvenirs such as papyrus, galabeyas, gold jewellery, leather goods, perfume, and spices. If you play your cards right you can get some good deals on these items compared to prices back home. However, don't spend all your holiday trying to beat the Egyptians down to the lowest possible price. I remember one holidaymaker asking how much I'd paid for my private taxi across to the Valley of the Kings and when I told him he seemed to gain great delight in telling me how he had managed to get one for 30 Egyptian pounds cheaper. But as I pointed out, maybe he had saved himself £3 but at least our driver was friendly and not disgruntled by having been browbeaten into accepting a lower price. You have to remember that 30 Egyptian pounds is a lot to an Egyptian. If you have agreed on what you think is a fair price don't start feeling aggrieved just because you heard someone else got a cheaper deal. It only leads to dissatisfaction and annoyance, which undoubtedly could spoil your whole holiday.

Tips and Tricks:

1. If you are with a partner there is a little trick that you can use. In Egypt, men are seen as the dominant sex (hmmm, I will say no more on the subject) and as such are treated with more 'respect'. Therefore, if you see something you would like to buy make sure that it is the female in the partnership that asks about the price of the item. Then, once the seller quotes a price, she should turn to her male companion and say 'do you like it?' At which point he should look totally disapproving and say something along the lines of; 'Why on earth do you want to buy that!"

Even if the Egyptian doesn't understand English, (and by the way, far more understand than let on) the seller will at least know from your partner's expression that he is not impressed and the seller will now feel under a certain amount of pressure to lower the price if he wants to ensure a sale. At this point the woman can now start haggling and the chances are, if you both continue to play the game well, you should end up with a decent price. (But don't overplay your hand, or try doing it at the next stall!)

2. Sometimes felt tip pens can also be used as bartering tools. Many shopkeepers have young children and if you have nearly reached a price for an item, but he is still hanging back, offer to throw in a couple of felt tip pens and it may just clinch the deal for you.

3. You can also say you have left most of your money on the boat for safety reasons. This works best if you make sure you have your 'budget' for the item in a separate pocket and pull it out, maybe making a point of counting it, as if you are uncertain how much you actually have left to spend. Last year i bought a lovely imitation shabti this way for a few pounds. Shabtis were small figures placed in tombs that pharaoh was able to call upon in the afterlife to do his bidding. Some of them are beautifully designed.

Small shabti funerary figurines designed to do manual labour in the afterlife

129

4. When shopping please note that smiling politely or making a joke does not always work in your favour as the seller often takes this as encouragement to continue. If you are unhappy with the attention the best course of action is to remain polite, disinterested and walk away. Be warned, if you look even the slightest bit undecided on an item, you will continue to be targeted, even followed. Once you get into the swing of things hopefully you will become more comfortable with the way things work and won't feel as pressured and start relaxing around the locals.

5. To get people off your back tell them you are going home tomorrow and you have no money left, emphasising it by pulling out your pockets (making sure of course that you have no money in them!) or giving an open handed gesture. Also slang words for 'no money' such as 'skint', 'broke' etc are widely understood. The traders usually take this in good humour and may even make a joke about it. I remember one particular seller looking at me with such feigned sadness before offering me (the poor little English woman) his can of coke. I couldn't help but laugh, as we both knew exactly the game we were playing!

6. Other avoidance tactics are to say you are feeling ill/sick. Or hurry through saying you are late for your coach.

7. Also try learning some basic Arabic phrases that will make sure you are clearly understood whilst browsing.

For example

ana bas bakhod felcra - I'm just looking

bikaam da - - How much is this

da ghaeli 'awi - It's too expensive

la' da kiteer 'awi - That's still too much

aekhir kalaem - Is this your best price

hashteree - I'll take it

hafakkar showaya - I'll think about it

bas keda shukran - nothing more, thank you

8. When you leave the boat on your own, taxi drivers will accost you. Whenever this happens do not be afraid to ask who is the cheapest. Then, if you find a taxi driver, guide, etc whom you particularly like then get his name and ask for him personally next time.

9. Not so much a tip but a suggestion. Haggling, which many westerners find extremely difficult to do, is a matter of attitude and in order to 'survive' you need to approach it as a challenge and not an ordeal! Simply learn from your encounters (and mistakes) and above all don't let it spoil your holiday. If you feel your temper rising - walk away. Remember don't be afraid to haggle, because believe me, Egyptian sellers aren't afraid to rip you off!

Scams: You will find children of all ages trying to sell you something, be it jewellery, papyrus bookmarks, little ceramic ornaments, plastic pyramids etc. On occasion some will give you an item for you to inspect and then refuse to take it back. In this

130

instance, if you do not want to purchase the item, simply put it down on the ground and walk away.

Adults do not tend to work in this way, but be wary of those asking if you would like them to take your picture. It has been known for them to refuse to give back your camera unless you give them money.

You will often have to run the gauntlet of traders at many of the ancient sites and towns. If they try to give you a 'free' gift do not accept, as this is merely a ploy to get you to buy something. It's best to politely refuse and carry on walking. Keep in mind, that vendors do not give something for nothing, whether in Egypt or England.

Con Artists: They are about and use various methods to get you to part with your money. Besides the above tricks, you should also watch out for;

Children who turn on the crocodile tears.

People who demand extra money because you paid up front. (E.g. it has been known for caleshe or taxi drivers to ask for more money to complete the return part of your journey)

People selling imitation goods. Such as papyrus made from banana leaves that break up within days. You can test if they are genuine by asking if you can roll them up before buying – if they split they are made out of banana leaves. Or cheap leather shoes / sandals made from camel rather than cowhide. Even saffron can be fake. You may see a huge bag at a very cheap price but unless you know what saffron looks like take care. Saffron should be fairly long strands about a centimetre long and coloured a deep orangey red. The strands should not be short and powdery. (I won't go into what it may be made from!)

Local tradesmen in the bazaars who will tell you that they work part-time on your boat, pretending to know you and asking why you don't recognise them. This is purely to make you feel guilty enough that you will buy something from their shop. They may even have a photograph of a boat that looks just like yours. I suggest you call their bluff by asking them the name of the boat you are travelling on. I bet they don't come up with the right answer! (By the way - if by sheer luck they do guess correctly, tell them they are mistaken.)

Watch out for the ones who also stop you on the street, asking, 'Do you remember me?' or 'Don't you remember talking to me yesterday?' Usually taken by surprise most people say, 'Yes, I think so...' And then before they know it they are being frogmarched by the elbow into a shop for the hard sell.

Local men who approach foreign men asking if they want a 'good time'. Usually this scam is set up in order to rob you. Do not go with anyone who comes up to you on the street, the same way, as you wouldn't just go off with a stranger if you were approached in the UK. Keep safe. Remember Egypt is a Muslim country with strict sexual laws.

Locals who say that a particular road is closed, or they know a quicker route and then take you via a bazaar where the shopkeeper pays them commission.

When paying for anything, including carriage rides or taxi fares, make sure you point out the money you are giving them. For example if you are paying with a 50LE, say so out loud as you hand the money over to them so they can not quickly switch the note for a similar looking 50 piastres note. This is a really common scam, which if they get away with it, will leave you 49.5LE out of pocket. Similarly if you are handing out several notes, count them out loud as you put them into their hand. If they still try it on, and you are confident that you gave them the correct money, hold your ground and let them know you are not pleased that they are trying to take you for a ride This will usually shame most of them into backing down. Do not become distracted by others, especially when dealing with large amounts.

Beware of taxi drivers that work in teams. Quite often a few may play the part of harassers, whilst one will act as the rescuer – seemingly coming to your aid by seeing the others off and thereby gaining your trust.

Watch out for those drivers who suggest you visit their homes. Usually they want to make you feel sorry for the conditions they live in so you will give them money or gifts. You may well also be told a sob story about how one of the family is at death's door and in need of urgent medical treatment.

Shopkeepers sometimes strike up friendly conversation during a sale hoping you will not notice that they have short-changed you.

Watch out for the unofficial bottled water sellers who have simply collected empty bottles and filled them for the domestic supply. This can easily be avoided by checking to see that the seal is intact around the cap.

Beware of people who would take advantage of your lack of local knowledge. This happened to us during our first trip to Cairo. After being dropped off by a taxi we were looking at a map to find the location of the antiquities museum when an Egyptian came up to us and asked if we needed assistance. We told him it was okay as we realised the museum was just round the corner. However, as he spoke excellent English, he started to strike up a friendly conversation, asking us where we were from, and how his wife was English and now taught in Cairo. I have to admit it was a very polished act and we were taken in hook, line and sinker. Then, when we were just about to take our leave he mentioned that the museum didn't actually open for another hour and if we wanted he had a shop not far away where we were more than welcome to pass the time. Uncertain, but not wanting to appear rude, we agreed, especially as he assured us he was not after any sale. Well, as you can imagine once we were in the shop we were presented with a couple of free cokes (a common practice), followed immediately by the hard sell! In the end, due to our naivety we spent about £50 on a papyrus and when we eventually returned to the museum it was to find it had been open all the time. So beware 'good Samaritans' - or Egyptians with gift shops!!

One small mercy at least it was a genuine papyrus of good quality and an original, signed by the artist.

The infamous papyrus!

It has to be said that scams and intimidation are more prevalent in Cairo than Luxor.

Intimidation:
This is by far the worst type of hassle and deserves no tolerance. Fortunately though, it is not a particularly common problem. When I say intimidation I mean those men who aggressively demand money with a threatening demeanour, and not those who just put out their hand as you pass by.

133

Again, I'm sorry to say that women are the most vulnerable and may be approached even within the Ancient sites if they are on their own. Above all, if approached do not give in to their demands for money. Stay calm, confident and look them straight in the eye whilst telling them to go away (imshi) And if that doesn't work, say you will call the police (*bolees*) if they don't leave you alone.

Unescorted women can also be subjected to sexual harassment and verbal abuse, particularly young girls, who may also be hassled by the local male youths. Arab women are generally helpful and will usually respond to a female in distress.

If you decide to do some sightseeing on your own, be aware of the men who say they must show you around the ancient site – that is not true. Tell them straight that you are looking around the site on your own.

It has also been known for some men to force their way into taxis around the various sites demanding to act as guides. If this happens refuse to be intimidated and decline their offer point blank. If he then refuses to leave, get your taxi driver to evict him. You will probably find that he will do this quite willingly, as he will be worried that you will not pay him!

I mentioned earlier about passing through the Esna lock and it was here on my first Nile cruise that I encountered intimidation for the first time. It was already getting dark when we reached the lock and like many others I decided to go up on deck to watch as we passed through and take a few photographs. Because there were several ships passing through at the same time we ended up in a queue and it was whilst we were waiting our turn that local men turned up in their boats selling goods. At this point the vendors started to throw up numerous cotton goods from below for inspection by the tourists. Just a short distance away, a woman who was similarly dressed was busy trying to agree on a price for a tablecloth. However, when things got a little heated the woman suddenly walked away when the boatman was distracted and unfortunately he then mistakenly started shouting the odds at me, saying I had stolen his goods and that he was going to inform the police. At first I tried reasoning with him calmly stating that I wasn't the same woman but no matter what I said he and his friends continued to throw abuse at me, until in the end I had to walk away due to their ever increasing aggressive and threatening behaviour. Needless to say I was very annoyed and more than glad to see the back of the lock as I half expected the police to board at any time.

One final note on this matter; I didn't tell this story in order to stop you buying from the boatmen, as I'm sure most of the encounters pass off without incident. By recalling this event I merely wish to make you aware that sometimes things can get a little out of hand, especially as this is a fairly unique situation where the vendor is some twenty feet below you and at a distinct disadvantage. As you will discover during further encounters, this disadvantage is a rare situation.

If you experience any sort of intimidation in any situation immediately tell your travel representative or travel guide.
Below I have included some Arabic phrases you could memorise. You can hear some of them spoken on our website where we also recommend various phrase books.
sebni fi haelee - leave me alone
hatemshi walla a Tlobi bolees - Go away, or I'll call the police
fi wahid biyedaye'ni - there is someone bothering me

FOOD POSIONING IN EGYPT
Having checked through many a hotel travel guide book in my time (including all the major tour operators) I find that most will try to persuade you that food poisoning is low down the list for causing stomach problems, but I have to say, from my own personal experience, it is the highest. Obviously the tour operators do not want you to think hygiene is not of the highest standard in Egypt and would prefer you to be the cause of your own illness. If you are still ill after returning home, e.g. any stomach cramps, loose motions, diarrhoea, sickness, intestinal discomfort then visit your doctor as soon as possible. Most likely you will be asked to provide samples to determine the cause of the infection, which could be either bacterial or viral. And remember to inform your travel company about any poor hygiene standards. Unless they are aware of the situation then nothing will change.
Egypt can be a bit of a culture shock at first and do not expect that health and safety and medical care to be up to western standards. However standards in most of the hotels and cruises are good and provide a decent service.
Stomach Upsets: I'm afraid there are no readily available scientific statistics I can offer regarding how many people fall ill with food poisoning whilst in Egypt, only my own experiences, which is; during my last nine visits to Egypt I became ill three times and all involved stomach upsets due to eating contaminated food. So in my case the chances were 33% in favour of you becoming ill. The first was in 1996 when the most I experienced was diarrhoea, which I quickly had under control. The second was in 2003, when I contracted non-specific food poisoning and suffered with gastroenteritis (diarrhoea, stomach cramps, sickness, and headaches). After a visit to a local chemist and using my own painkillers, I was up and about again within thirty-six hours. The third time was in 2009 when I contracted salmonella poisoning, a notifiable disease for which I claimed against the travel company as my holiday was basically ruined. The symptoms were similar to gastroenteritis but with an added severity including near collapse, aching all over (especially my joints) and lethargy. My stomach and intestinal pain started to decrease and eventually stopped after

135

some 6-8 hours so I knew I was getting better. I had become ill three days into the holiday and was unable to do anything but stay in the room for the rest of the week. I didn't seek medical advice in Egypt, which with hindsight was probably foolish, and instead starved myself for 48 hours, drinking only water and black coffee, which I thought would kill off the bug. (So much for that theory) After that I ate very little, namely toast for breakfast and the emergency food I'd packed in our cases, which I knew I could trust. The most important thing is to keep yourself hydrated. The flight home was a bit of a worry, but thankfully I made it without any mad dashes to the toilet.

On return to the UK I continued to have severe attacks of sickness, diarrhoea and hot and cold sweats on a three-day cycle that left me on the verge of fainting. After a week I provided stool samples to my doctor and was diagnosed with the bacterial infection salmonella. If you are still feeling ill when you get back home don't leave it as long as I did, but get yourself along to the doctor as soon as possible. Besides salmonella other common infections you can pick up in Egypt are campylobacter, cryptosporidium, Ecoli, Dysentery/Shigella. All these infections are caused by poor food hygiene and handling practices.

Examples of the main sources of contamination are;
- Poor food hygiene practices by cooks, kitchen and waiters causing cross contamination.
- Handling of food without gloves by kitchen staff
- Food not properly cooked (e.g. chicken, eggs, fish, beef)
- Food dishes not kept hot enough
- Cold food left standing too long and uncovered
- Pool contamination from infected guests
- Dirty conditions in bathroom (e.g. leaking toilet)
- Unhygienic cleaning methods
- Ice cubes (if not made from bottled water)
- Certain fruits that have already been peeled

At the end of the day there are no guarantees, so it's simply a case of weighing up how much you want to visit Egypt, compared to the chances of you becoming ill. Still, for those of you who would like more advice I've compiled the list below. How far you take this is entirely up to you.

Suggestions to help protect against illness;
- Eat only HOT food (e.g. soups, toast, rice, main meals) and avoid salads, pasties, ice creams, cheeses and cold meats
- Arrive at the beginning of mealtimes, not towards the end as some of the dishes may have been stood for a long time and either cooled down (if hot) or warmed up (if originally cold).
- When spooning food out of the tureens look for the hottest spot so you get the hottest food on your plate.

136

- Don't have ice in your drink
- Wash your hands after handling Egyptian money as this can be a source of infection.
- Clean teeth with bottled water only
- Always have a shower after using either the ship's swimming pool or Jacuzzi.
- Carry antiseptic wipes in your pocket or bag, especially when out and about.
- Wipe all taps down with antiseptic wipes before using
- Wipe all toilet seats down with antiseptic wipes before using
- Wash your own hands regularly
- I take antibiotics with me in case of toothache but I know some people take them in case of food poisoning. (However many diseases are no longer treated with antibiotics as doctors believe they actually prolong certain infections, such as salmonella.)

TRAVEL INSURANCE:
It is extremely important that you do not travel to Egypt without adequate medical insurance and make sure it covers the costs of hospitalisation and medical repatriation to your own country. If your argument is that you can't afford travel insurance, then you can't afford to travel - no matter how fit and healthy you are. The standard of medical facilities in the main cities is adequate for routine conditions but away from the cities, facilities are very basic. Treatment can be expensive and the vast majority require payment in advance. In the event of serious illness or accident, evacuation to better facilities may be required, so medical costs can be considerable. Keep your insurance details with you, including policy and telephone numbers.

Now for a little known problem that I feel you should be made aware of regarding travel insurance.

Whilst booking my Egyptian holiday online in 2009 I was asked if I wanted to take out travel insurance at the same time and as the price seemed quite reasonable I decided to go ahead.

However, whilst away I fell ill with salmonella poisoning and as I could prove unequivocally that I had only eaten at the hotel where we stayed I decided to make a claim on my insurance for our ruined holiday.

And that's when I found out there was a problem.

Apparently because the travel insurance company was in partnership with the travel company through whom I'd booked my holiday, I was not entitled to submit a claim because, as it was clearly pointed out to me, 'We would effectively be suing ourselves and we can't do that!'

So buyer beware, when taking out travel insurance make sure you purchase it separately through an independent company or you may fall foul of the same rule.

Luckily I was covered by my house insurance who, after asking me to provide them with some basic information, determined that I stood a good chance of winning and agreed to take on my case.

It took awhile, over twelve months, before the travel company finally accepted responsibility and I received compensation. But it was worth the wait as within two weeks I was back in Egypt in order to carry out the research I needed for this new edition. And I didn't suffer a single stomach upset all week!

If you do fall ill on your holiday and you believe it is the travel company's fault, as they endorsed the cruise ship or hotel, then the best advice I can give you is to collect as much evidence as possible in order to prove your case.

Regarding illness, if you're on a cruise you will not need to prove in as much detail where you ate, as all meals are usually provided by the boat, however if any part of your holiday is spent in a hotel, say on bed and breakfast or half board terms, then where you ate and what you drank becomes far more relevant to your claim, hence the need to keep all receipts.

Whether you suffer illness or an accident immediately inform your rep of your condition and get them to fill in a signed incident form and get a copy. Also, I highly recommend you keep a detailed diary, not only from the time of your illness but from day one, so you can easily recall events if asked to, in order to prove your case, such as what you ate or drank at different mealtimes. Remember illness and accidents can strike at anytime so better to be prepared from the start. Besides, it will give you something to do whilst you're sat lazing around the pool soaking up the sun, and provide you with a nice memento of your holiday, and also help organise your photos when you get home. ☺

It should be noted, that like mine, the vast majority of claims do not go to court.

I have included a section at the end of this book 'Illness and Minor Accident Claims' which you may find useful as it offers advice on what to do to help support any claim.

TERRORISM THREAT

Visitors should be aware that there is a high threat of terrorism in Egypt and I'm afraid no one can issue any guarantees of safety. Although security is tight throughout the country, especially in resort areas, Egypt does lie next to a troubled region of the Middle East and shares a border with Israel. Attacks can be indiscriminate and against civilian targets, including holiday resorts. Because of this Egypt remains one of a number of countries where there remains a threat from international terrorism.

Tourists are easy targets because;

1. Holiday-makers are usually on a package deal, which means they have predictable schedules, making attacks easy to plan.
2. By killing tourists the terrorist hit the government economically.

138

Whilst Egypt's tourist trade has undoubtedly suffered over the years from these abominable acts, it still remains surprisingly resilient and demonstrates the human resistance not to give in to bullies.

My advice - if you are of a nervous disposition and are constantly worried by 'what may happen to you', then you really need to consider if Egypt is the ideal holiday destination for you, as such concerns could probably ruin your holiday.

Egypt's security forces are making considerable efforts to ensure the safety of foreign visitors, with the police now insisting on escorting travellers to remote areas. In the past there had been attacks on the desert road from Aswan to Abu Simbel but since the authorities started accompanying the coaches their presence has deterred further trouble.

However, the risk of indiscriminate terrorist attacks against civilian targets, including places frequented by foreigners, means you should remain vigilant at all times and exercise caution in your daily activities – especially around crowded tourist areas such as Cairo.

Travellers are advised to visit their Foreign Office website for the latest information. I have included a list of Egyptian terrorist attacks at the end of the book.

CIVIL UNREST
RIOTS, DEMONSTRATIONS AND PROTESTS

Protests and riots do happen in Egypt and it is something you need to be aware of. Reasons for the demonstrations are varied, including religion, (particularly between Muslims and Christians), food shortage, low wages, high prices, poverty, education and health issues, unemployment, football, and anti-government protests. Unemployment is high in Egypt, around the 25% mark, with a rate of 76% amongst its youth. Many Egyptians earn less than 40LE (£4 or 7US$) a day and an average family of seven will live in one room.

If you get caught up in any form of protest or demonstration whilst in Egypt, no matter how peaceful they may seem, use your common sense and make a swift exit!

Do not get involved with local politics, do not pass comment, offer your opinion, or join the protestors, just be sensible and make your way back to your cruise boat or hotel immediately, following any instructions given to you by officials or your travel company representative.

Do not be tempted to go and see the demonstrations for yourself.

Stay in your accommodation area, keep away from crowds and observe any curfew.

25th JANUARY 2011 RIOT:

As I write, Egypt is experiencing some of its worst riots as thousands of Egyptian people have taken to the streets in protest against the current government that has been in power for 30 years. This popular uprising have been fuelled by the recent revolution in Tunisia and by the Internet generation who have been called to arms by a 'Facebook' page setup in the memory of 28 year old Khaled Said who was beaten to death by the Egyptian police in June 2010.

Tahrir (Liberation) Square, set back from the Nile lies at the heart of the capital and has become the focal point of the protestors and the bloody battleground for Egypt's future. Thousands have set up camp there with people from all walks of life joining the demonstrations; wealthy, poor, educated, illiterate. The protestors are demanding the immediate resignation of President Mubarak and want assurances that his son will not run in elections due later this year. They believe the government and police are highly corrupt and want Egypt to become a truly democratic country. Although the army is present, they remain impartial, acting mainly as a deterrent to violence. The internet has been taken down, along with several independent TV stations and telecommunication systems. Even though Mubarak has offered concessions and promised to leave after the next elections, it is not enough for the people who want complete freedom from his 30 year authoritarian rule.

The British Foreign Office has advised against all but essential travel to Egypt and is urging people not to travel to certain cities, including Cairo, Luxor, Alexandria and Suez. Obviously this is a very worrying and anxious time for the estimated 30,000 plus British tourists currently in Egypt. It's reported that large numbers have already made their way to Cairo Airport in an attempt to leave the country as the unrest continues. Many ancient sites have been closed by the military including the pyramids and the Cairo Museum.

1st February 2011: Billed as 'The Million People Day', anti Mubarak demonstrators called for the masses to descend on Tahrir Square to show their support, which they did en masse. The whole day was spent in a party atmosphere, with the army remaining neutral.

2nd and 3rd February 2011: After 18 hours of prolonged fighting in Tahrir Square, during which time over 100 people died, the anti-government protestors finally beat back the pro Mubarak supporters who probably rely upon the regime for their salaries and perks. The army, which is held in high esteem by the general public, is now caught between the president, who himself is an ex-military man, and the populous. However the army generals have said that they will not attack the protesters. But neither did they play a huge part in helping to break up the violence, much to the anger of the anti-government protestors. Still, Mubarak refuses to resign.

Many believe the battle for the square was a turning point.

11th FEBRUARY 2011:
RIOTS THAT BECAME A PEOPLES REVOLUTION.
After 18 days of protest that has seen 300 people killed and over 3000 injured President Hosni Mubarak has finally resigned and handed over power to the Supreme Council of the Armed Forces, who have promised reform and to end emergency rule. The army is now expected to steer the country to free and fair elections with no delays or rigged ballots. All over Egypt there have been jubilant celebrations as people are now able to visualise a brighter future with the sweeping away of one of the longest surviving Arab rulers. But they also realise it is only a battle partly won as they want a true democracy without the army at the helm, which means an unknown period of huge instability. Throughout the day the stage was occupied by members of the opposition, all politically jockeying for what comes after Mubarak and a place in history.

SUMMARY:
Mubarak is the second Arabic president to be deposed in as many months and the repercussions will be felt far wider than the shores of Egypt, with many old-guard unelected Arabic rulers being rattled by the revolutions. As the most populous Arab nation Egypt is vital to the stability of the whole region. As president, Mubarak helped to maintain the fragile peace treaty signed in 1978 with Israel and won the friendship of the west, which included a yearly two billion dollar aid programme from the US.
What the west and Israel fear the most is an anti-western political party coming to power, such as an Islamic fundamentalist group.
The world is now closely monitoring the situation in Egypt which could prove a pivotal turning point with consequences that, as yet, are unpredictable. How this political earthquake will affect future tourism has yet to be revealed. But what we can be sure of is that Egypt will never be the same again.
For the first time in 8000 years the Egyptian people, without conspiracy, without organisation and for the main part, without violence, have said what they want and have been heard. For what must be an exciting, but uncertain time for them, I wish them well.
I will post regular updates on the situation via our website.

TRAVEL SAFETY
The vast majority of the incidents and accidents in Egypt do not involve Nile cruise tourists, however as many tourists return to stay in hotels and tour independently, I thought it best to include them for future reference.

RAIL: Egypt has a comprehensive rail network and there is a high standard of rail service available to tourists and Egyptians who can afford it. However as in many developing countries, rail safety for the poor is not well funded and most Egyptian passengers are packed into cramped compartments on old, slow trains. Plus passengers on long-haul journeys often carry large amounts of baggage, take small animals onto the train and prepare their own meals, sometimes using portable gas cookers. Egyptian trains are often filled way beyond capacity and there have been terrible accidents in the past. As far as I am aware, no tourists have been killed in any reported major accidents. A list is included at the end of the book.

ROAD: Egypt has one the highest traffic accident rates in the world. According to official government estimates some 8,000 people die and 32,000 are injured in road accidents each year in Egypt. Many of the fatal crashes are due to speeding, reckless driving, poorly maintained roads, poor vehicle maintenance and a lack of enforcement of traffic regulations with many drivers ignoring road signals and signs. The US State Department warns on its website that travelling on Egyptian highways can be dangerous and even prohibits its Embassy officials from travelling outside Cairo after dark because of driving hazards.

I've experienced several incidents myself including a Cairo driver who decided the best way around the traffic was for him to mount the kerb and drive along the pavement, narrowly missing several pedestrians. A taxi driver we hired to take us to El Fayoum had such bad eyesight that we had to keep warning him about dangers ahead. A mini-coach driver, taking us from Luxor to Hurghada, who constantly overtook on bad bends, only narrowly avoided several collisions by a hair's-breadth, and a coach driver travelling from Aswan to Abu Simbel who fell asleep at the wheel! If it hadn't been for the quick reactions of the tour guide who grabbed the steering wheel I hate to think what might have happened! If you're unhappy with the way a vehicle is being driven you should firmly instruct the driver to slow down, or make your feelings known to any accompanying tour guide. Nearly all the major accidents listed at the end of this book included the death of tourists.

BALLOON FLIGHTS:
For many years hot air balloons have been rising over the early morning skies of Egypt offering tourists spectacular aerial views of the West Bank. However in 2009 flights were suspended after an accident in which 16 tourists were injured, some seriously. On the 24th April, a pilot took off without permission in rough weather and collided with a mobile phone tower, causing the balloon to crash some 30 feet to the ground, hitting power lines as it plunged downwards. As it hit the floor, the balloon was dragged along the ground, spilling passengers out of the basket.

The crash was not without precedent. The winds in April can reach 100mph, and last year seven tourists were injured in a similar incident. Besides weather problems, ballooning is also hampered by overhead cables and pylons and further hemmed in by the Valley of the Kings now being strictly off limits.

142

Within 48 hours of the accident all balloons flights were suspended and the government insisted that all pilots would have to be retrained, no matter how good their safety record was. The government also introduced numerous measures aimed at preventing further accidents. For instance, all take-offs are now under the control of the world's first hot air balloon 'airport', not far from the famous Colossi of Memnon and it was decided that no more than 8 balloons would be allowed up at any one time. Previously, anything up to 50 could share the same air space, which was potentially very hazardous. The threat of a hefty fine if they land their balloon in the wrong place has also given an extra incentive for all pilots to perform well.

Six months later, on the 26th October 2009, the ban was finally lifted and the balloons once again took to the skies. As a previous 'flier' who thinks the balloons are a great experience, I am pleased to see them flying again, plus the improved regulations will undoubtedly reassure the public that they are in safe and capable hands. Thankfully, there have been no further balloon accidents. However the downside of all this re-training and less availability is that the average cost of a 30-minute trip has nearly doubled from £65 to £120 per person!

Balloon over Medinet Habu

RIVER:

Since a tragic felucca accident, that happened last year, 2010, many travel companies now issue you with a foam padded lifejacket whilst onboard any small boat. Most people choose not to wear them, but that is a personal choice. For those who can't swim, or are afraid of water their presence will be reassuring. The safety record of the large Nile Cruise ships is generally good as proven by the listed accidents at the end of the book.

AIR:

Egyptair is the flag carrier airline of Egypt and is state owned. It is the largest African airline, operating passenger and freight services to more than 80 destinations. I have flown with EgyptAir and have no complaints. However there have been a number of fatal accidents which are recorded at the end of this book.

143

RED SEA:
Accidents and incidents in the Red sea are rare. However last year the popular holiday resort of Sharm el-Sheikh was badly affected when the area suffered from a number of shark attacks. The beaches were re-opened on the 13th December 2010 with special measures being introduced by the authorities to safeguard tourists. From now on hotel owners will have to adhere to new controls to ensure the safety of foreigners while diving or swimming. New watch stations manned by divers are to be set up and speed boats will continuously patrol the waters. Swimmers will also have to remain within designated areas. Experts have speculated that overfishing in the area may have driven sharks closer to shore, whilst other believe sharks could have been drawn to the area after a ship carrying sheep and cattle for sacrifice during the Muslim festival of Eid al-Adha dumped the carcasses of dead animals which had died during the voyage.

CRIME RATE

ROBBERY: Of all the Arab countries Egypt is still considered to be one of the safest with crime and acts of violence against tourists quite rare. After all, without the tourists many Egyptian livelihoods would suffer greatly, as foreign tourism accounts for 10% of its gross domestic product. However, whilst incidents of violence are low, petty crime, such as pick pocketing and purse snatching does occur, especially around the market areas. If you do go to the souq be very careful with your handbag. Usually one man may try to distract a woman whilst another rifles through her bag. Just keep your wits about you, your bag fastened and secure against your person.

Valuables such as cash, jewellery and electronic items should not be left unsecured in your room or left unattended in public places. Remember expensive watches, mobiles and cameras make tempting targets so avoid taking them to Egypt. (I only take costume jewellery) Make use of your cabin safe and lock larger valuables in your suitcase. Victims of crime must report it to the tourist police (white uniform) immediately, as failure to do so before you leave Egypt could affect any claim or prosecution.

For safety reasons I suggest you make copies of your passport, tickets, and travellers cheques before you leave and keep them in your locked suitcase, so you can provide details should you have them stolen.

SEXUAL ASSAULT: According to the UK foreign office website,
<Quote> '*We continue to receive a significant number of reports of cases of sexual assault cases against British Nationals. In 2009, we handled 26 cases of sexual assault and three cases of rape. Some assaults were against minors. Many occurred in what were considered to be safe environments e.g. hotel premises.*'
</Quote>

Women travelling on their own, particularly when using taxis, are more prone to harassment therefore I would advise you not to let them know you are alone, but give the impression you are in Egypt with your partner who is currently 'feeling unwell' in your cabin or room.

To help put this into perspective 1,346,724 British Nationals visited Egypt in 2009 and I have included this information mainly to make people aware of the possible dangers and the need for personal and parental vigilance. Always take sensible precautions as you would in your own country, especially if you are a woman travelling alone, or you have children with you.

NILE POLLUTION

As you visit Egypt and sail the Nile you will not help but notice the pollution in the river, especially around the main towns such as Cairo, Alexandria, Luxor and Aswan. Just looking over the side where the boat moors you will see rubbish either floating on top of the water, at visibility level just below the surface, or piled up against the riverbank where it has been deposited.

In 2006 a report by the 'World Bank' said river pollution in and around the Alexandria and Greater Cairo areas were unhealthy. According to the report, pollution in the Nile is caused primarily by urban wastewater discharges and industrial effluent. They suggested that toxic effluent is harmful to both fish and humans. The World Bank report went on to say that poor water quality was affecting people's health, agricultural productivity and fisheries. It also stated that, Egypt's population increased from 36 million in 1973 to 66.4 million in 2002 and is expected to reach 86 million by 2020. The rapid population growth coupled with ambitious development and industrialization policies have put a heavy pressure on Egypt's natural resources in the form of severe air, water and soil pollution. It reported that, 'Egypt's track record for implementing and enforcing environmental laws has not been very successful. With limited exceptions, violations of environment-related laws went undetected and requirements were often not enforced, especially with the public sector polluting enterprises.'

The World Bank reports stated that in the Nile Delta faecal coliform bacteria counts are 3-5 times higher than elsewhere in the country. More recently another study commissioned by the independent daily newspaper 'el-Masri el-Youm' found concentrations of harmful materials like phenol (carbolic acid), cyanide, ammonia and nickel were higher than national and international permissible standards.

The Egyptian government is highly concerned and has taken measures with the Egyptian Environmental Affairs Agency (EEAA) to gradually expand its functions and responsibilities in all fields of environmental water management at a national, regional and local level.

145

However in June 2009, Maged George, Egypt's Minister of Environment, announced during celebrations of the World Environment Day, that according to the government's annual report, drinking water pollution had reached "complex stages that are difficult to be faced" and that the extensive number of bodies managing water resources has obstructed a solution. The report also cited 129 industrial facilities and 300 floating hotels (cruise ships) that were pumping chemical and other waste into the Nile and that excessive use of fertilizers and pesticides was another major source of water pollution despite the success in considerably reducing the level of use of agro-chemicals during the past decade. It was acknowledged that many challenges still remain; including the fact that about only one third of the population is connected to sanitary sewers, which means a lot of untreated wastewater is released into the Nile. The low level of sanitation service especially in rural areas makes nearby streams (either canals or drains) the perfect places for inhabitants to dispose of their sewage. Another problem was the poor operation of facilities, such as wastewater treatment plants.

As you can see from the above, it isn't surprising that the Nile is suffering from the consequences of such action and whilst improvements are being attempted there is still a huge way to go as pollution continues to constitute an uphill struggle for environmentalists and water experts. I have no doubt that the pollution problems facing the Nile, which were very much in evidence during my last visit, 2011, will persist for some time.

DISABLED FACILITIES

I have to be perfectly honest and say that facilities for the disabled in Egypt are very poor with amenities on most ships non-existent. How badly this will affect your holiday will depend entirely on the severity of your disability. If moderate, i.e. able to walk on your own with the aid of a stick or aided by another person, then generally speaking most of the ancient site visits and activities, in theory, should be accessible to you. However for those of you in a wheelchair then the prospects are not as rosy. Having asked cruise tour guides if they cater for people in wheelchairs they say they can, but that it isn't easy, and I have to admit during my many trips to Egypt I have never seen a wheelchair bound person on any of the Nile cruises.

However that isn't to say that it doesn't happen, as I am aware of one 5-star boat (MS Amarco) that is fully adapted to accommodate wheelchair passengers, with two lifts giving full access to all four decks, a separate lift accessing the sun deck, exceptionally spacious cabins and fully adapted bathrooms. It also has a purpose built ramp to give access to the riverbank in Luxor. But one fully equipped boat out of 300+ cruise ships is not a very good track record.

Probably the best way to demonstrate what any disabled or mobility restricted person is up against on any regularly fitted out cruise ship is to show you the obstacles you will undoubtedly encounter whilst on ship, out and about in the towns and at the sites. This information is for reference to those of you not wanting to book through a travel company that caters specifically for the disabled.

BOATS AND EMBARKATION:
The average Nile cruise ship is usually a four or five level boat with no lifts, just stairs.

Compact shower room

147

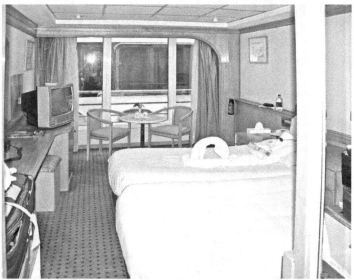

Cabin area is at a minimum

An average two bed cabins is fairly compact with little room to manoeuvre a wheelchair. Bathrooms are fairly small with no mobility aids such as rails, handles or grab bars and frequently

148

have cramped triangular shower units. Corridors and doors are quite narrow. Access on and off the boat is via a narrow gangplank with the vast majority being loose rope sides (not solid handrails).

Access to the main roads from where the boat is moored is via stone steps up a steep gradient of up to twenty feet. The condition of some of the areas can be rough and rocky. The quay shown is at Komombo and is one of the less-steep inclines. Ramp access is not available.

These riverside areas can also have obstacles such as mooring ropes, chains, tools and pipe work for water, sewage and diesel etc strewn across them, which can make their negotiation awkward for those with walking difficulties.

Usually several boats moor alongside one another, and at times you may have to cross over several boats (can be up to seven) to get to land and their entrances do not always line up so some tricky manoeuvring between ships is required. The crew and attendants on the ship will lend a helping hand.

Typical steep sided embankments with gangplank at Kom Ombo

Many of the ancient site visits involve early morning starts; which can create difficulties for the less mobile who may need time to let their bodies 'loosen up' after getting out of bed.

OUT AND ABOUT:
The majority of roads and pavements are not always in the best of conditions, with many potholes, broken tarmac, exposed cables, cracked or lifted flags and huge kerb stones with no dropped wheelchair access. Crossing roads can be pretty hair-raising as vehicles rush towards you without slowing down and simply toot

149

their horns madly, basically telling you to get out of the way. Bad enough for able-bodied persons believe me!

Sometimes crossing the river in order to visit some of the ancient sites involves the use of motorboats or feluccas (sailing boats), none of which are brilliant for people with any degree of mobility problems. Staff will help you cross the narrow plank but it can still be an effort to climb down onto the decking and maybe have to clamber over a central seating panel in order to get a seat.

High black and white kerbs - present throughout Egypt

Accessing the small motorboats for visits to the West Bank can be precarious

Boats moored up against each other. Sometimes up to seven ships have to be negotiated in order to reach the quayside.

VISITING ANCIENT SITES:

Some of the sites cater better for disabled persons than others. For example both Karnak and Luxor temples are more or less on the flat and you should have no difficulty visiting these, with wheelchair users needing the minimum of assistance.

To a lesser degree the Valley of the Kings is okay, although a little tough going since the path is mostly gravel, not paved and with an incline.

Internally tombs are more difficult and can involve steps and/or steep ramps and maybe some bending. Because of this only certain tombs will be accessible, for example Ramses IV tomb is ramped, providing wheelchair access quite deep inside. Unfortunately accessibility does not include Tutankhamun's tomb which involves descent by steps.

If your mobility problems are not too severe then you may manage most of the tombs, especially if you do your research and choose your tombs carefully.

If you book a day trip to Cairo then again the pyramids, sphinx and Museum of Antiquities will require some help for wheelchair users, but not those of moderate disability or incapacity. However access inside the Great Pyramid is problematic.

Sites which will prove more difficult are the Aswan quarries and Philae Temple. The former involves a steep climb up many steps and over rock, whilst the latter is a motorboat ride with a difficult landing in a very busy area. Whilst not impossible, they will take a certain amount of organising and physical exertion.

151

The unfinished obelisk site at the Northern Quarries of Aswan

You will encounter steep steps during the obelisk climb

The pictures above will help you evaluate the climb around the unfinished obelisk. If you decide against the ascent you can wait near the new visitors centre under the shade of a tree.

CONCLUSION:
Getting around the sites is not always easy, even for those with a moderate disability. A person in our group had a bad hip and it bothered him so much that by the end of the week he could no longer walk without great discomfort and had to curtail many trips. My advice would be to take any walking aids you normally use, a good pair of flat shoes (ones that you've already broken in, not new ones), a large supply of anti-inflammatories, pain killers, prescribed medication, muscular heat rubs and even a hot water bottle.

The drive for better accessible travel opportunities in Egypt has largely come from overseas tour operators who specialize in packages for disabled travellers but progress is slow and still very much in its infancy. For example, even though Egyptian law stipulates that five percent of hotel rooms should be handicapped accessible, in reality, this is not always the case.

If you search on the internet you will find holiday companies offering trips to Egypt for disabled persons, both hotel and cruise based, and whilst they try to accommodate people with all levels of disability they usually ask that you contact them first to discuss your requirements and any equipment hire such as; commodes, shower chairs, hoists, scooters, adapted taxis and adapted excursions. Some also offer nursing and medical assistance. Because these are bespoke packages, created to suit individual requirements you are unlikely to get a 'brochure price'. When booking I would suggest you only use those companies who have good reviews, a proven track record and are recommended for their consistency in services.

Philae arrival and departure point involving steps and motorboats

HORSE WELFARE IN EGYPT

You may be appalled by the poor condition of some of the horses who pull tourist carriages (Caleshe) in Egypt. Many have body sores, infected eyes and are generally emaciated.

You may also witness mares who have their foals strapped to them as they are forced to run around the cities. In the heat, some of these poor animals look ready to drop. The drivers tend to gallop

153

the horses and use their whips unnecessarily. It can be a heartbreaking sight. Rarely do you see a horse in the shade or drinking.

Just this year, during the riots in Tahrir Square Cairo, Egyptian Horses were ridden into the middle of the protest with little thought for the welfare as they were pelted with rocks and sticks. It must have been very distressing and frightening for the animals.

If you do decide to use a caleshe try to hire one who obviously looks after his horse and if possible let the other drivers know why you have chosen that particular carriage, then hopefully the conditions for the mistreated horses will improve.

Do not hire them to take you to the West Bank; the distance is too far for the horses. Get a taxi instead.

There is an equine welfare charity called the Brooke which currently helps over 100,000 working equine animals in Egypt alone, by providing free veterinary care, training and education for millions of owners via a network of mobile veterinary teams and community participation. In particular, the charity focuses its attention on the carriage owners of Luxor, Aswan and Edfu in order to improve the conditions of the horses.

The Brooke was founded in 1934 by Dorothy Brooke, who was shocked at the plight of the horses she encountered on a visit to Egypt and with donations from the British public she bought 5,000 of these exhausted animals and went on to set up the first free veterinary clinic, the 'Old War Horse Memorial Hospital' in Cairo, which still operates today.

The Brooke's enthusiasm and hard work continues to help and improve the lives of thousands of working horses, donkeys and mules in some of the world's poorest communities. Last year alone, they helped over 740,000 working animals.

Caleshe outside Luxor Temple

PHOTOGRAPHY AND CAMCORDER RESTRICTIONS

For the past few years the Egyptian Antiquities Authority has been tightening up on what you can and can't photograph. Personally I am really annoyed by the unnecessary restrictions.

Places that you can NO longer photograph include;
- Valley of the Kings (Including exterior and internal shots)
- Any museum (including the Museum of Antiquities at Cairo where all Tutankhamun's treasures are housed and the royal mummies)
- The inside of any pyramid
- The interior of any tomb
- The interior of the Abu Simbel temples
- Aerial shots of the Valley of the Kings from a balloon flight

The way things are going I can see it won't be long before the interior of all temples will be on the no-go list! And then what - no photography whatsoever?

Whilst I have sympathy with the inappropriate use of flash in the tombs, with regards to the delicate colours being affected, I have always thought that those disregarding this rule were never chastised enough by having their pictures either deleted or their film confiscated. And instead the authorities have taken the easy route by banning all cameras and camcorders which effectively punished us all, rather than the few who flout the rules.

Nor do I understand why you can't photograph the outside of the tombs in the Valley of the Kings or the inside of any museum. After all, the British Museum has no such restrictions and they have just as many precious artefacts.

All hot-air balloons have now been stopped from passing over the Valley of The Kings, (the main tourist site on the west bank) so you must content yourself with photographing some of the lesser monuments from the air.

The main sites where there are presently no restrictions are the temples of Karnak, Luxor, Kom Ombo, Edfu and Philae, plus the mortuary temple of Deir el Bahri (Hatshepsut) and the Colossi of Memnon. Let's hope this list doesn't get any shorter.

THE TRUE COST OF YOUR HOLIDAY

Extra costs which will not be included in your holiday price are; extra trips, visa, general tips, staff gratuities, additional excursions, bottled water, cruise photographs and videos, your tour guide's fee, internet connection, photo transfer onto DVD, taxi fares, souvenirs, costume for Egyptian party, plus drinks tab if you are on full board, so you will need to budget accordingly.

It's amazing how quickly the cost mounts up with all the hidden extras you aren't told about. In light of the above I would suggest you have a credit card handy for emergency funds. (Credit card payments are usually subject to a 2.5- 3% surcharge.)

EARLY STARTS AND INTERRUPTION TO SCHEDULE

Schedules can change at the drop of a hat. For example last year we actually set sail for Edfu the day after we arrived, which meant we did the Luxor visits at the end of the week rather than the beginning. This would have been ok, except we were booked on the one day trip to Cairo, which meant we had to do the west bank visit on the day of departure.

So when others were doing the Valley of the Kings etc, we were up at 4am and around the pyramids by 9am. Unfortunately there was a hold up with our return flight which meant instead of getting back to our boat at 11pm, we arrived back at 1am and then had to be up again at 5am in order to cram in our Valley of the Kings tour, whilst others were packing. We were exhausted and barely had a couple of hours sleep.

Occasionally and with little warning, the water level of the Nile can vary, which in turn can affect itineraries. This is caused by the Egyptian authorities altering the flow of water from Lake Nasser.

Esna lock used to close for routine maintenance twice a year, usually June and December, and when this happened the cruise ships start their journey from Esna, rather than Luxor. However for the past three years it has been continuously open. How long this will last, I have no idea. I tried to find out through various sources without any luck, so all I can suggest is that you definitely ask at the time of booking whether or not the situation has changed.

If you are booked on a balloon trip be aware you will have to get up very early, around 4am in time for your sunrise flight, which is ok, as long as the balloon takes off, which sometimes doesn't happen due to weather conditions. If this happens to you, you will be expected to do the same again the following day, and the next, until you manage to get up. The tour and balloon companies do not like to give refunds and will keep trying until they get you up in the air, no matter how tired you are!

MOORING

Due to numbers, ships usually moor up against one another.
This can;

1. Greatly restrict your view
2. Necessitate the closure of your curtains
3. Restrict the opening of your window
4. Greatly diminish available light
5. Increase noise
6. Increase the smell of diesel
7. Cause a claustrophobic feeling
8. It may involve you walking through one or more vessels before you reach the bank.

This is a particular problem in the busy season. If you feel hemmed in I suggest you take yourself off to the sundeck where at least you will be able to see daylight. I would say close mooring can account for 40% of your week's holiday. Just keep your fingers crossed that you are one of the outer boats.

The oppressive closeness of a ship next to the window makes it dark

A Cautionary Tale:
One night around 9pm our boat was moored up in Luxor. There were many people on the sun deck enjoying a drink and chatting when another ship arrived and began to manoeuvre in towards us. It was already dark and as the boat drew closer people began to watch and admire the skill of the captain as he gently glided the boat up against us. Their ability is quite phenomenal and a pleasure to observe.

However as the ship drew closer it was obvious that a certain cabin's occupants were totally unaware that their ship was docking and still thought they were merrily cruising the Nile away from prying eye as their curtains were wide open, the light on and the woman was completely naked!

As news spread more people came out of the bar to watch the free show and even the Egyptian waiters, who you usually had to send out a search party to find, were suddenly in abundance, trying to look as they weren't looking, but obviously were.

Eventually word must have gotten down to the other ship's reception who telephoned the couple, because the man now aware of what was happening swiftly closed the curtains, effectively finishing the show to the consternation of many of the men onboard.

Thinking that was the end of it, many went back to the bar but suddenly the curtains were flung open again and the woman, whose modesty was now covered with a towel, smiled, blew several kisses and gave a little curtsy, much to the amusement and admiration of her remaining audience, who clapped and cheered.

I have to give her credit, if that had been me, I would have been utterly mortified and probably wouldn't have come out of my room for the rest of the week.

So, you have been warned to close your curtains at night as these boats are very manoeuvrable and the vast majority of the pilots so good at their job, that unless you are actually looking out of a window, or you're on deck, you won't necessarily know when your boat is docking.

Hopefully after reading this you won't wake up one morning to find the locals peering through your cabin window due to the ship having moored during the night. ☺

Ships moored up in a row

NOTE: Due to printing restrictions the photographs in this book have only been produced in standard 8-bit greyscale, therefore if you wish to see colour versions and other imagery please visit our website at:

http://www.travel-egypt.co.uk/colour.php

SUMMARY

As I mentioned at the beginning, this book should be used as a general guide as every cruise will have its own itinerary, entertainment programme and food menu. What I have tried to do is give you the most popular sites and activities that you may come across, plus a few personal insights into the way things work.

Having read this book you may be thinking – is Egypt for me? The problem with writing a 'telling you how it is' book is that the negatives can appear to outweigh the positives. However, to put things into perspective I have to reiterate that in all probability the worst you will encounter on your holiday is pestering from the local Egyptians who work the tourist areas. Whilst this hassle is annoying, you just need to get used to saying, 'No thank you' (La'a shukran) without thinking you are giving offence.

It's also worth remembering that a cruise will cushion you against most of the nuisance we've mentioned and besides, the magnificent ancient sites will more than make up for any hassle you may encounter. ☺

I firmly believe that Nile cruises are the best introduction to Egypt as they provide excellent value for money and access to sites that you may miss out on during a hotel based holiday. Plus, it is the most enjoyable way to view the country for the first time, as you glide up and down the river from the comfort of your ship.

I have heard it commented that a cruise may be 'too touristy for them' but in my opinion it is still the easiest way to get a feel for the land and the ways of the people, so hopefully by the end of your holiday you will know if you would like to return and visit other areas like Cairo and the pyramids.

The purpose of this book is not to discourage you from travelling to Egypt but to promote interest in the wonderful Ancient Egyptian culture and hopefully to encourage holiday-makers to choose a Nile Cruise. To put things into context, I have been travelling to Egypt for over two decades without incident and will continue to do so because of my love of the history of the land and the fact I never tire of the awe-inspiring sites and majestic Nile.

I hope you have enjoyed reading this as a small flavour of what to expect during your Nile Cruise and as the saying goes, 'Forewarned is forearmed'. ☺

The next section contains useful information regarding current prices, holiday check list, money conversion chart, offers, lists of gods, symbols, myths, Arabic phrases etc. Plus a few blank pages at the end of the book where you can write your own notes.

If you decide a Nile cruise is for you, then have a fantastic time and should you wish to contact us please feel free to drop us a line at; info@travel-egypt.co.uk. We look forward to hearing from you.

PRICE LIST
In Egyptian Pounds (LE)

Below are some common prices for 2011. However please bear in mind that prices are always subject to change and this list should only be used as a rough guide. Plus it has been muted that site prices may increase by 30% towards the end of 2011.

GENERAL

Bottled water (2 litres – off the boat)	5
Beer (pint)	50
Toilet paper (2 sheets) at public toilets (i.e. Valley of Kings)	1
Internet Use (30 minutes)	40
Internet Use (60 minutes)	60
Photo transfer to CD	45
Taxi (per taxi - one way – full length of resort)	25
Felucca (per person, per hour)	25
Doctor (1 visit)	300
Prescription	40

SOUVENIRS

Musical Toy Camel	100
Nefertiti Snow Globe (small)	40
Nefertiti Snow Globe (large)	80
Pack of Photos from various sites	50
Postcards	5
Glass Perfume Bottle (small)	30

SOUTHERN SITES
(Most of which will be included in your holiday package)

Valley of Kings (3 tombs)	80
Tutankhamun's Tomb	100
Ramses VI	50
Hatshepsut's Temple	30
Karnak Temple	65
Luxor Temple	40
Luxor Museum	80
Mummification Museum	60
Edfu Temple	50
Kom Ombo	30
Unfinished Obelisk	30
Philae Temple	50
High Dam	20

NORTHERN SITES

Giza Plateau	65
Entrance to 'The Great Pyramid' (Khufu)	100
Egyptian Antiquities Museum	80
Mummies Room at the Museum	100
Solar Boat Museum	60
Saqqara	60
Dashur	30
Meidum (Sneferu)	40

160

HOLIDAY CHECK LIST

HOLIDAY PREPARATION
• Holiday Insurance
• Passport (check expiry date and blank pages)
• Relevant Visa (Can be purchased on arrival)
• Foreign Currency/Credit Cards/Travellers Cheques

HOLIDAY ESSENTIALS
• Prescription medication
• First aid kit:
   Plasters (all sizes and on reel), antiseptic cream, insect
   repellent, sting relief, painkillers, calamine lotion, safety pins,
   diarrhoea medications, muscular heat rub, indigestion
   tablets, scissors, needle and cotton, antiseptic wipes,
   rehydration sachets, cotton pads, cotton wool, lint, tweezers,
   small magnifying glass, bandages (support, stretch and normal),
   paper hankies, thermometer, lip balm (or Vaseline), antiseptic
   throat lozenges, smelling salts, Vick rub
• High factor suntan lotion
• Sunglasses and sun hat
• Pocket torch and batteries (better still, manual wind-up)
• International electrical socket adapter

PHOTOGRAPHIC EQUIPMENT
• Camera(s) and relevant storage media (e.g. memory cards)
• Interchangeable lens for SLR (if appropriate)
• Camcorder and storage media
• Batteries and chargers
• List of photographs required for each site

OTHERS YOU MAY WISH TO CONSIDER
• Mobile Phone and Charger
• Travel Kettle
• Portable DVD and media
• Your own pillow
• Extension cable
• Fan (Foldable, hand-held)
• Travel Games
• Spare pair of spectacles or contact lenses
• Food and drink
• Travel Guides and site maps
• iPod/mp3 player/portable CD player and media
• Writing material

EGYPTAIN HIEROGLYPHS

On this page you will find the common signs and symbols used by the artisans and scribes of the temples.

Depending upon which book you are referring to, you may find there are various hieroglyphs for different letters - sometimes even two or three.

Below we have given, what we consider, to be the most popular.

EGYPTION MYTHOLOGY

This section is provided just to give you a taste of a few of the many myths and legends that colour the history of Ancient Egypt and to add interest to the sites you will visit.

CREATION MYTHS

There are actually four different creation myths in Ancient Egypt, below are two of them.

1. THE ENNEAD (from the Hermopolis region – Lower Egypt)

According to the Heliopolis doctrine, the solar god Atum was born on a mound known as the ben-ben that rose out of the water of chaos known as Nun. Atum was the sum of all existence and using either masturbation, spittle or his blood he became the father of Shu and Tefnut. They in turn were the parents of Geb and Nut, whose children were Osiris, Isis, Seth and Nephthys. Together these nine gods made up the Heliopolitan Ennead. After the lord Atum, the four deities, Shu, Tefnut, Geb, and Nut established the Cosmos, whilst their four children were the communication between heaven and earth. This meant that all future gods and pharaohs were descended from those nine deities. This legend came from the Old Kingdom and was popular until the Ptolemaic period.

2. THE OGDOAD (From the Memphis region – Lower Egypt)

In this ancient creation myth it was said that the Ogdoad created a mound that rose from the primeval waters and on this they formed an egg from which the young sun god, Ra, emerged.

The Ogdoad was made up of four pairs of deities, (one male, one female) each embodying a different aspect of the primal world:
Nun and Naunet, the god and goddess of the primordial waters;
Kuk and Kauket, the deities of darkness;
Amun and Amaunet representing invisible power;
Huh and Hauhet representing infinity.
The females were associated with snakes (rebirth) and the males with frogs (fertility).

Later in the New Kingdom period Atum and Ra would become associated together as 'Atum-Ra', in order to cement the two creation beliefs.

THE STORY OF OSIRIS AND ISIS

The goddess Nut had five children. The first born was her son, Osiris, followed by Horus the Elder, Seth (lord of evil), Isis and her second daughter Nephthys. When Osiris became a man he married his sister Isis and Seth married Nephthys a common custom in

Egyptian mythology. Osiris became sole ruler of Egypt and taught his savage people how to cut the flesh of suitable animals, how to plant seeds, cut the corn when it was ripe, and how to thresh the grain, dry it and grind it to flour and make it into bread. He showed them how to plant vines and make the grapes into wine and how to brew beer from barley. Osiris then went on to teach them laws, and how to live peacefully and happily together, delighting themselves with music and poetry. Soon Egypt was filled with peace and plenty and Osiris set out over the world to bring his blessings upon other nations. While he was away he left Isis to rule over the land, which she did both wisely and well. However their brother, Seth the Evil One, detested and envied them both. The more the people loved and praised Osiris and the happier mankind became, the stronger Seth's desire to kill his brother grew. Secretly Seth obtained the exact measurements of the body of Osiris and had a beautiful chest made that would only fit him. It was fashioned of the rarest and most costly woods and exquisitely decorated. Then Seth, in league with 72 of his followers gave a great feast in honour of Osiris with the choicest of foods, the richest of wines and the most beautiful dancing girls ever seen. When the heart of Osiris had been made glad with feasting and song the chest was brought in and all were amazed at its beauty. Osiris marvelled at the rare cedar inlaid with ebony ivory, gold and silver and the painted inside showing figures of gods, birds and animals, and he desired it greatly. 'I will give this chest to whosoever fits it most exactly!' cried Seth. And every man began in turn to see if they could win it, but everyone was either too tall or too short, too fat or too thin for the chest until Osiris laid himself down. 'I fit exactly. The chest is mine!" he cried. 'Indeed it is yours and shall be so forever!' hissed Seth as he banged down the lid and in desperate haste nailed it shut and sealed every crack with molten lead. And so Osiris died.

Seth then had the chest cast it into the Nile where Haapi the Nile-god carried it out into the sea where it was tossed for many days until it came to rest on the shores of Phoenicia near the city of Byblos. Here the waves fashioned it into a tamarisk tree that grew on the shore and the tree grew beautiful leaves and fragrant flowers making it a fit resting place for the body of the noble god Osiris. Very soon the tree became famous throughout the land and when King Malcander heard of it he gave orders that the tree should be cut down and formed into a great pillar for his palace. This was done and all wondered at its beauty and fragrance but none knew that it held the body of Osiris.

Meanwhile in Egypt Isis was in great fear. She had always known that Seth was filled with evil and jealousy but had not been able to convince Osiris of their brother's wickedness. As soon as Isis knew her husband was dead she fled into the marshes of the delta carrying their baby son, Horus with her. She found shelter on a little island where the goddess Buto lived and entrusted the divine child to her. And as a further safeguard against Seth, Isis loosed the island from its foundations and let it float so that no one could tell where to find it. Once her baby was safe she set off on her journey to seek out the body of Osiris, for she knew until he was buried with all the necessary rituals and charms his spirit could not enter the hereafter.

Back and forth over the land of Egypt she wandered but never a trace could she find of the chest in which lay the body of her husband. She asked all whom she met, but no one had seen it and in this matter her magic powers could not help her. At last she questioned some children who were playing by the riverside and they told her of such a chest that had floated past them on the swift flow and out to sea. Because of this, Isis blessed the children and decreed that ever after children should speak words of wisdom and sometimes tell of things to come. At length Isis came to Byblos and sat down by the seashore, in the guise of a peasant woman. Presently the maidens who attended Queen Astarte, wife of Malcander, came down to bathe at the water's edge and after engaging in conversation Isis taught them how to plait their hair, which they had never seen done before. Whilst engaged they told her about the wonderful tree that had suddenly started to grow on the shore. Isis immediately understood then that the tree was in fact her husband's coffin that had floated ashore. When the maidens went back to the palace the Queen marvelled at their plaited hair and asked them how it had come to be done so. The maidens told her of Isis and she immediately sent for her, asking Isis to serve in the palace and tend her children; the little Prince Maneros and the baby Dictys, who was quite ill. Astarte was totally unaware that this strange woman was the greatest of all Egyptian goddesses.

Isis agreed and very soon the baby was strong and well and she had become so fond of the child that Isis thought to make him immortal, which she did by burning away his mortal parts. Astarte, however, who had been watching her secretly, rushed into the room with a loud cry when she saw that her baby seemed to be on fire and so broke the magic. Then Isis took on her own true form and Astarte crouched down in terror when she saw the shining goddess and learned who she really was. Malcander and Astarte offered her gifts of all the richest treasures in Byblos but Isis asked only for the great tamarisk pillar which held up the roof. When it was given to her, she caused it to crack open and took out the chest. The pillar she gave back to Malcander and Astarte where it remained the most sacred object in Byblos, since it had once held the body of a great god.

Isis at length placed the chest on a ship which King Malcander provided for her and set sail for Egypt where she hid the chest in the marshes of the delta while she hastened to the floating island where Buto was guarding her son, Horus. By chance Seth was in the area, hunting by night for wild boars with his dogs, as was his custom since he loved the darkness in which evil things abound. By the light of the moon he saw the chest of cedar and immediately recognized it. At the sight hatred and anger welled up inside him and he tore open the chest, took the body of Osiris, and ripped it into fourteen pieces which, by his divine strength, he scattered up and down the whole length of the Nile so that the crocodiles might eat them.

And so Isis' search began once more but this time she had helpers, for Nephthys left her wicked husband Seth and came to join her sister. And Anubis, the son of Osiris and Nephthys, taking the form of a jackal, assisted in the search. When Isis travelled over the land she was accompanied and guarded by seven scorpions, but when she searched on the Nile and among the many streams of the delta she made her way in a boat made of papyrus and the crocodiles, in their reverence for the goddess, touched neither the rent pieces of Osiris nor Isis herself.

Slowly, piece by piece, Isis recovered the fragments of Osiris and wherever she did so she formed by magic the likeness of his whole body and caused the priests to build a shrine and perform his funeral rites. And so there were thirteen places in Egypt which claimed to be the burial place of Osiris. In this way she also made it harder for Seth to meddle further with the body of the dead god. Only one piece of his body was not recovered, his penis, for it had been eaten by the Oxyrhynchus fish (sturgeon) which Isis forever cursed.

Isis however, in order to fool Seth, did not bury any of the pieces in the places where the tombs and shrines of Osiris stood and instead gathered them together, rejoined them and by magic created a phallus so that Osiris was complete. Then she embalmed the body, wrapped it in bandages and hid it away in a place which she alone knew. By doing so Isis had made Osiris into the first ever Egyptian mummy. After this the spirit of Osiris was able to pass into Amenti (The Underworld) to rule over the dead until the last great battle, when his son Horus should slay Seth and he would return to earth once more.

When Horus was grown he gathered his forces together and prepared to begin the war against Seth in order to avenge his father's murder. There were many battles in the war, but the last and greatest was at Edfu, where the great temple of Horus stands to this day in memory of it. The forces of Seth and Horus drew near to one another among the islands and the rapids of the First Cataract of the Nile. Seth, in the form of a red hippopotamus of gigantic size, sprang up on the island of Elephantine and uttered a great curse against Horus and Isis.

'Let there come a terrible raging tempest and a mighty flood against my enemies!' he cried, and his voice was like the thunder rolling across the heavens from the south to the north. At once the storm broke over the boats of Horus and his army whilst the wind roared and the water was heaped into great waves. But Horus held

166

on, his own boat gleaming through the darkness, its prow shining like a ray of the sun. Then, opposite Edfu, Seth turned and stood straddling the whole stream of the Nile, so huge a red hippopotamus was he. But Horus took upon himself the shape of a handsome young man, twelve feet in height and in his hand he held a harpoon thirty feet long with a blade six feet wide at its point of greatest width. Seth opened his mighty jaws to destroy Horus but he cast his harpoon and it struck deep into the head of the red hippopotamus and deep into his brain. And that one blow slew Seth the great wicked one, the enemy of Osiris and the gods. The red hippopotamus sank dead beside the Nile at Edfu. The storm passed away, the flood sank and the sky was clear and blue once more. Then the people of Edfu came out to welcome Horus the avenger and lead him in triumph to the shrine over which the great temple now stands. And they sang the song of praise which the priests chanted ever afterwards when the yearly festival of Horus was held at Edfu. 'Rejoice, you who dwell in Edfu! Horus the great god, the lord of the sky, has slain the enemy of his father! Eat the flesh of the vanquished, drink the blood of the red hippopotamus, burn his bones with fire! Let him be cut in pieces, and the scraps be given to the cats, and the offal to the reptiles! Glory to Horus of the mighty blow, the brave one, the slayer, the wielder of the Harpoon, the only son of Osiris, Horus of Edfu, Horus the avenger!'

Osiris, Isis and Horus

167

But when Horus passed from this earth and ruled no more as the Pharaoh of Egypt, he appeared before the assembly of the gods, and Seth came also in spirit, and contended for the rule of the world.

Seth put his case so well, that not even Thoth the wise could give judgment, therefore Osiris was declared king of the Underworld, Horus king of the living, and Seth ruler of the deserts as the god of chaos and evil.

And so it comes about that Horus and Seth still contend for the souls of men and for the rule of the world. There were no more battles on the Nile or in the land of Egypt and Osiris rested quietly in his grave, which (since Seth could no longer disturb it) Isis admitted was on the island of Philae, the most sacred place of all.

Nevertheless the ancient Egyptians believed that the last battle was still to come and that Horus would ultimately defeat Seth and when he was destroyed forever, Osiris would rise from the Underworld and return to earth, bringing with him all those who had been his faithful followers. And this is this reason why the Egyptians embalmed their dead and placed the bodies beneath pyramids and deep in the tombs, so that the blessed souls returning from the Underworld would find their bodies ready to enter again so they could live forever on earth under the rule of their beloved Osiris, Isis his queen and their son Horus.

THE COBRA AND ITS ROLE IN ANCIENT EGYPTIAN MYTHOLOGY

You will find the symbolic female Cobra is often repeated in long friezes in temples and tombs throughout Egypt, denoting the importance of the snake in Egyptian mythology.

The hooded Cobra is the most feared of all poisonous snakes. At an average length of six feet, with a brownish skin, glaring eyes, darting tongue, hissing breath and spoon-shaped hood, it rates as one of the most dangerous snakes in the world. Worshipped since the beginning of man's history its name is synonymous with myth and legend.

The cobra is a silent, stealthy hunter, which feeds on insects, lizards, frogs and small mammals, such as rats and mice. The ancient Egyptian stored much grain in their temples and palaces and undoubtedly these areas would have been infested with rats and mice, which probably ate up to 15% of the supply. And where rats were, the Cobra was bound to follow.

The cobra lives approximately 20 years, shedding its skin as it grows. To the ancients it must have looked miraculous, as if the Cobra was capable of rebirth. Hence its strong connection with Pharaoh, as he to, was thought to be immortal.

Although it does not seek attention, once confronted, the Cobra will be roused into a vicious defence. The venom is an extremely complex protein, which the Cobra injects into its victims

168

bloodstream. Even when decapitated it has been known for the head of a Cobra to still be capable of biting and killing for some while after.

Even given its dangerous properties the Cobra still remains the favourite of snake charmers. From ancient times these people have put their lives at risk. They know their snakes well and exactly how far they can manipulate them. It is not the music of the snake charmers flutes that catch the attention of the Cobra, as the snake can only hear low frequency sounds and ground vibration, but rather the movement of the flute and the snake charmer himself that draws the snake into its aggressive posture.

In ancient Egypt every 'healer' was required to know the repertoire of spells for conjuring the poison of every serpent. Snake-bite victims would be given a concoction of herbs, oils, plants extracts etc, whilst charms and spells were recited to protect the victim, his friends, family, and the healer himself.

Obviously the healers of ancient Egypt sometimes got it right and the remedies did work. But this was probably due more to the fact that a Cobra does not always inflict a fatal injection, rather than the practitioner's skills.

Originally the Horned Viper, known in ancient times as 'Fu', was regarded as the Royal Serpent of the Egyptian Pharaoh and early kings would often have the snake's name as part of their own, e.g. Khu-fu, Shepsesku-fu. However in later Egyptian history, during the solar religious period of Ra, the Cobra replaced the Viper as the Royal Serpent and came to represent the burning eye of Ra.

It is thought that the different properties between the snakes venom may have played a part in this transformation as there is evidence that the Cobra may have been used on occasion as the instrument of death for the king or queen, as in Cleopatra's case.

Certainly when you compare the slow, painful death caused by the horned viper whose venom attacks the blood causing it to slowly clot, with that of the Cobra, whose venom attacks the victim's nervous system causing a relatively swift death by suffocation, then you can see the reasoning behind the change.

The ancient Egyptian goddess Wadjet, the female Cobra, had her chief shrine in the marshes of the Delta. Wadjet was the protector of Pharaoh, aggressive and always ready to attack the enemy. Pharaoh would often wear a representation of the wide hooded Cobra on his forehead as an emblem of royalty. From this position Wadjet was said to defend the king, either by spitting venom or by a burning flash from her eyes. In the Pyramid Text the uracus, an enraged female cobra was said to rear up and spit flames, which consumed rebels.

The 'Crown of the South' (red crown) worn by Pharaoh bore the Cobra and was known as the 'Lady of Dread'. However when combined with the 'North Crown' (white crown) which also bore the Royal Vulture, the Cobra was referred to as the 'Lady of Flame'.

169

Lady of Flame

In the 'Book of the Dead' the Cobra is seen as the symbol of Earth.

The Ouroborus sign shows a snake swallowing its own tail bringing together circle and serpent representing totality, rebirth, immortality and the round of existence.
The earliest known written referral to the Ouroborus is contained in the tomb of Unas at Saqqara. Whilst the Dama Heroub papyrus, a 21st dynasty scroll, contains one of the oldest depictions of an Ouroborus.

EGYPTAIN GODS

There are many Egyptian tales of creation including that of Heliopolis, Hermopolis, Memphis and Thebes and each have their own set of gods. But the confusion doesn't stop there as throughout Egypt's long history gods were often reinvented, renamed, became associated with other gods, or had their characteristics completely changed. So don't be surprised if one god's information conflicts with another. For example Atum, Nun Ptah, and Amun are all listed as the world's creator, simply because different myths arose in different regions and dynasties. Below are some of the most popular. Alternative names are in brackets.

Ammut (Amemait, Ammam Ammit):
Ammut was an ugly female demon god from the Underworld who took care of the punishment of sinners. She had a crocodile's head, front part of a lion or panther (or both) and the rear of a hippopotamus. All of them were dangerous animals feared by the Egyptians, so put together they were terrifying. Ammut sat at the Osiris Court when the heart of the deceased was weighed against the feather of Ma'at. If the heart was heavier than the feather then the deceased was a sinner and Ammut would swallow it, causing the soul of the departed to be forever restless. Thus one of her names was 'The Devourer'. Her main cult centre was at Thebes.

Amun (Amen, Amon): 'God of War' or the 'Hidden One'. A deity strongly associated with Thebes and Karnak Temple where he is described as the 'King of the Gods'. He became assimilated with Ra, the most powerful sun god. There are many representations of Amun, including the ram, goose, frog-headed and in anthropomorphic form with two tall plumes on his head and a sceptre in his hand. His main cult centres were at Thebes, Hermopolis and Magna.

171

Anubis: In primitive times Anubis, the jackal god, was associated with the dead because the jackal was generally seen prowling about the tombs. His worship is very ancient and may be older than that of Osiris. In the Unas pyramid text (Book of the Dead) at Saqqara, he is associated with the Eye of Horus and his duty was that of guiding the dead through the underworld to Osiris. Again in the Funeral Procession scene Anubis receives the mummy and, standing by its bier, lays his protecting hands upon it. The duty of guiding the souls of the dead around the Underworld and into the kingdom of Osiris was shared by Anubis and another god, Ap-uat, whose symbol was also a jackal. Known as the Guardian of the Necropolis, he was also a patron of magic and it was believed he could foresee a person's destiny. Anubis was also the god of embalming and the keeper of poisons and medicines. It is written that he provided the ingredients (herbs, powders and unguents) to help Isis and Nephthys embalm Osiris. Anubis then performed the funeral of Osiris, which would be the role model for all funerals to come. As part of the funerary ritual he would perform the 'Opening of the Mouth' ceremony before the mummy was put into the tomb. This ensured that the deceased would be able to speak in the afterlife. In the "Hall of Maat", it is Anubis who sees that the beam of the great scale is in the proper position as he supervises the weighing of the heart of a deceased person against the feather of Ma'at to determine whether a person was good or evil. Anubis also protects the dead from Ammut, 'The Devourer'.

Anuket (Greek- Anukis): In the old kingdom Anuket was an ancient goddess of the Nile in areas like Elephantine Island and the first cataract were the river starts its journey through Egypt. Originally she was a goddess of Nubia. Since the god Khnum and goddess Satet were thought to be the gods of the source of the Nile, Anuket was believed to be their daughter. As a huntress she became associated with fast-moving things, like arrows and the deer. She is often depicted as a gazelle, or a woman with a gazelle's head. Other times she is a woman wearing a tall crown of reeds and feathers, grasping a papyrus staff. When the Nile started its annual flood, the Festival of Anuket began. People threw offerings into the river, thanking her for the life-giving water. Her chief religious centre was on the island of Seheil where she has a temple.

Apep (Apepi, Aapep, Greek – Apophis):, Apep was an evil god, the personification of darkness and chaos and the opponent of light and truth. Apep was usually seen as a giant snake or serpent and was viewed as the greatest enemy of Ra, who slayed him most nights as he travelled through the underworld. In their battles, Apep was thought to use a magical gaze to try and hypnotize Ra and occasionally he got the upper hand causing thunderstorms, earthquakes and eclipses.
But in other myths, it was the cat goddess Bast, daughter of Ra, who killed Apep, hunting him down with her all-seeing eye.

Apis: The sacred bull of Memphis. Apis is a form of Ptah-Osiris and recognized by the blaze on his forehead and the sun disc between horns on his head. Real bulls were sacrificed at Sakkara in honour of the god and buried in a special tomb area known as the Serapeum.

Aten: The sun god, shown as a sun disc with emanating rays that ended in hands. This god was the invention of Pharaoh Akhenaten who wanted to do away with the polytheism society of Egypt and replace it with monotheism, the belief in a single, all-powerful god. He managed for a number of years but after his death, the old ways of multiple god worship was reinstated by the priests who had lost a huge amount of power during the Aten period. The main cult was at Akhetaten, Amarna. The origin of

173

monotheism is unclear, but Akhenaten's attempt is the first recorded in history.

Atum: The great creator god of Egypt with his main cult centre at Heliopolis. He is represented in many forms including, a man with Nemes headdress, a human leaning on a stick, a black bull, snake, or just as a crown. Later he was to become associated with Ra.

Bastet (Bast, Ubasti): Bastet was the goddess of Bubastis in the Delta region, whose symbol was a cat. The exact meaning of her name remains uncertain but one suggestion is 'She of the Ointment Jar' as her name was written with the hieroglyph 'ointment jar' (*bȝs*) and she was associated with protective ointments. The picture above shows Bastet on top of an ointment jar. In the old kingdom she was a protector goddess of pharaoh and was usually depicted as either a fierce lioness or a woman with the head of a lion but later she was changed into a cat goddess rather than a lioness.

Bes: Bes is a fat bearded comical dwarf figure that is always shown face on, never in profile, which is quite unique in Egyptian art. There are also depictions of Bes with feline or leonine features. He is often shown sticking out his tongue and holding a rattle. Bes is the patron of the home, childbirth, infants, humour, song and dance. He was particularly loved by the masses as he as thought to bring good luck and happiness to homes.

174

Geb: Geb was an Earth and fertility god and a member of the Heliopolis Ennead. It was believed that his laughter was earthquakes. Geb was the son of the earlier primordial gods Tefnut and Shu and father to the four lesser gods Osiris, Seth, Isis and Nephthys. Geb was mostly shown as a man reclining beneath his sky goddess wife, Nut. As history progressed, the deity became more associated with the habitable land of Egypt the underworld and with vegetation, with barley being said to grow upon his ribs. Consequently he was depicted with other plants on his body.

Hapi (Hapy): This god was regarded as the 'Spirit or Essence of the Nile'. The annual inundation (flooding) was the arrival of Hapi. It was believed he had a cavern in the first cataract of the Nile at Aswan from where he discharged the rising waters. Along with Nephthys, Hapi guarded the canopic jar, which contained Pharaoh's lungs and whose stopper was the head of a baboon. He is often depicted as a well-fed man with pendulous breasts, a headdress of Nile plants and carrying a heavily-laden table of offerings.

Hathor (Greek Aphrodite): An Old Kingdom goddess of Heaven, Earth and the underworld. She was known as Horus' wife. She had many titles, including The Golden One'. Hathor is closely associated with music, joy, the desert, and sexuality. The 'Seven Hathors' were the goddesses who decided the future of any new borne. Her cult was worshipped at Dendera, Luxor, Sinai and Memphis. She is often depicted as a cow, or a woman with ears and eyes of a cow, or a woman with wig, horns and sun disc, or with a falcon perched on her head. Even today in the south of Egypt a man may say to a woman, 'You have the eyes of a cow.' Meaning she is beautiful. One of the most powerful goddesses Hathor is often associated with Isis and the Greek goddess, Aphrodite. Her name means 'House of Horus'.

Hor-sma-tawy (Ihy, Greek - Harsomtus): He was the son of Horus and Hathor and his name means, 'Horus Uniter of the Two Lands'. His main cult centre was at Dendera where he was the heir apparent of the divine kingdom. He is often depicted as an infant suckling at his mother's breast. He was also a god of music and could be shown as a boy with a side-lock of hair (denoting youth) and carrying a sistrum.

Horus: The 'Protector of the Reigning King'. The large impressive temples of Edfu and Komombo are dedicated to Horus. As the son of the god Osiris and Isis, he became known as the ancestor of all pharaohs. Pharaoh was often referred to as 'Horus, the living God on Earth'. In Egyptian mythology Horus is associated with both the sun and moon and is usually depicted as a falcon, hawk wearing a crown, or a man with a hawk's head and either a sun disk or crown on his head. Horus is the god of Kingship.

Isis (Aset): 'Goddess of Many Names' / 'Queen of the Gods'. Isis was the most popular Egyptian goddess, even though her true origins are in doubt. However, it is generally believed that she was worshipped in the Delta region, close to Busiris, the oldest known cult centre of Osiris. She had close associations with every great Egyptian goddess, including Nut, Bastet, and Hathor. Isis played a prominent role within the relationship of the gods. She was known as the daughter of Ged and Nut, the sister-wife of Osiris, the mother of Horus and the sister of Seth and Nephthys.

Along with Neith, Selket and Nephthys she is one of the four goddesses that guarded a corner of any royal sarcophagus with outspread wings.

Under her particular protection was the canopic jar containing Pharaoh's liver. Both Isis and Nephthys were known as the chief divine mourners at Pharaohs funeral. But she is most famously known in mythology for her quest to find her murdered husband's body. Throughout the legend Isis typified the faithful wife and devoted mother. Her magical powers, particularly in the care and cure of children, ensured her continuing popularity. (See the 'Egyptian Mythology' section for the full story)

Isis took on particular importance during the Ptolemy reign (30th Dynasty) when several temples were built in her honour including the temples at Dendera and Philae. The worship of Isis continued through both the Greek and Roman occupations of Egypt, up until the sixth century AD. During this time Isis was universally worshipped and her cult had spread through many lands including; Syria, Palestine, Asia, Cyprus, Crete, Rhodes, mainland Greece, Phoenicia and eventually Rome. The worship of Isis even spread as far as Britain.

Isis is often depicted nursing her son Horus, or with outspread wings, a sign of protection, as on Tutankhamun's sarcophagus, or with a throne shaped headdress.

Khnum (Khnemu): A ram-headed god of the Cataract region was one of the earliest Egyptian deities. He was the consort of Anuket and Satet. As a creator god he was thought to have created man on his potter's wheel from clay. He was worshipped in Elephantine, Esna and Nubia.

Khonsu (Khons): Khonsu was a god of the moon, time and knowledge. His cult centre was at Thebes where he was part of a triad with Amun and Mut. It was thought that he could influence the fertility of the people and their livestock. He was also revered as a god of healing. Regarded as one of the companions of the god Thoth,

Khonsu was a great lover of games and is frequently shown playing Senet with Thoth. He is also shown as a youth with a side-lock of hair, staff in his hand, horns and a moon disc on his head. He has attributes of a demon expeller.

Ma'at (Mayet): The Goddess of truth and justice who had cult centres throughout

Egypt. The goddess represented the ideals of law, order, balance and truth. The word, Ma'at translates into 'That which is straight'. She is a daughter of Ra and the wife and female counterpart of Thoth. Ma'at is a very ancient goddess and is sometimes called the 'Eye of Ra' or the 'Daughter of Ra'. Ma'at also plays an important part in the Book of the Dead and it is in the 'Hall of Ma'at' that the judgement of the dead takes place by weighing the purity of their heart against the feather of Ma'at. If the heart and feather balance then they are deemed worthy of entering into the afterlife. If the heart of the deceased was heavier it would be devoured by Ammut and the soul of the person would be destroyed forever. Ma'at is often represented as a woman with outspread wings, wearing a tall ostrich feather on her head. Or, just as an ostrich feather.

Min (Amun-Min): God of Fertility, thunder, storms and the desert. As one of the most ancient of Egyptian gods he is probably pre-dynastic. He is particularly associated with two ancient cities - Gebtu and Khent-Min where he was worshipped in the form of a white bull, a symbol of virility. As a desert deity he became associated with nomads, travellers and hunters. Later, in the 18th dynasty he became linked with the most powerful of gods, Amun (Amun-Min) and is usually depicted as a man with a phallus denoting his connection with fertility. He had his own harvest celebration - 'The Festival of the Coming Forth of Min'.

Mut: Lady of Heaven. In the New Kingdom she acquired the position as a primeval goddess, called: "Mother of the Sun in Whom He rises". Mut was both the eye of the sun and the mother of the sun. The goddess was regarded as the mother of pharaohs. According to myth, she was self-created. As a vulture goddess she was often shown as a woman with a vulture on the crown of Upper Egypt. Mut was also depicted as a woman standing with her arms stretched out with a large pair of wings. The goddess

178

became the Eye of Ra when Amun was in the position of the sun god, and in her association with the goddess Sekhmet she was represented as a lioness. Her temple was situated at Asheru, a suburb of Thebes.

Nefertum (Nefertem): Is a god of healing born in a lotus. The lotus from which he emerged became associated with him. He is the son of Ptah and Sekhmet. Nefertum appears as a man wearing the lotus and two plumes on his head. Sometimes he is shown with a lion's head. One story says Nefertum brought Ra a sacred lotus to ease his suffering.

Neith: The deity of Sais in the Delta region. A very ancient warrior goddess depicted as a woman wearing the red crown of Lower Egypt and carrying a bow and arrows. She became one of the four goddesses that protected the dead and watched over the sarcophagus and canopic jar containing the stomach. She was also accredited with the invention of weaving.

Nephthys: She is the sister of Isis, Seth and Osiris. She also married Seth. She is one of four guardian goddesses of the dead and watched over the canopic jar containing the lungs. According to some fables she is the mother of Anubis. Often depicted as a woman wearing a basket shaped headdress.

Nun: One of the eight original creator gods known as the Ogdoad. He was a frog-headed god who arose out of the waters of chaos together with his consort Naunet, who had a serpent's head. Together with the other six gods they created the world. Also seen as a man holding a solar barge above his head, or a baboon.

Nut: Nut according to legend is the daughter of Shu and Tefnut and the wife of Geb, the earth god. Representations show her bent over the earth as the connection between heaven and night. Sometimes she is a cow straddling the earth. Her body is usually sparkling with stars. It's said she swallowed the sun each night and gives birth to it each morning. According to myth she gave birth to four children, Osiris, Isis, Seth, Nephthys and sometimes five, when 'Horus the Elder' is included.

Osiris: (Ansur) Was the main god of the Underworld. The constant battles between Osiris and his brother, Seth, were the basis for the Egyptian account of the creation. The eventual death of Osiris, caused by this sibling struggle, enabled the Afterlife to come into being. As the principle god of the underworld and the judge of the dead, he represented order and justice in the next world and was the supreme ruler. It's thought that Osiris probably started out as a harvest god, due to his Atef crown. One of his principle cult centres was at Abydos. He wears the insignia of royalty with crook, flail and Atef crown with plant stems and ostrich feathers. He is usually presented in mummy form. As judge of the dead he appears in both the 'Pyramid Texts' - the oldest collection of religious spells known to us from ancient Egypt, and the 'Book of the Dead'. Osiris, like Isis is universally revered.

Panebtawy: Panebtawy was the divine child of Horus and Tasenetnofret and was worshipped at the temple of Kom-Ombo as a child god. He was known as 'The lord of the Two Lands' and represents the idea that pharaoh as the living son on Earth of the god Horus, hence the legitimate ruler of Egypt.

Ptah: A creator god and one of the oldest. According to legend it was Ptah who called the world into being, by speaking it out loud. His name means 'opener' in the sense of 'opener of the mouth' and it's said that Ptah created the 'opening of the mouth' ceremony performed by priests at funerals to release souls from their corpse. Another story says Ptah is the creative potter-god shaped the world and heavens assisted by the seven wise worker-dwarfs of Khnemu. Ptah is portrayed as a bearded mummified man, often wearing a blue skull cap. In his hands he holds an, ankh, 'was' scepter and djed, the symbols of life, power and stability. It was also considered that Ptah manifested himself in the Apis bull, a revered animal in ancient times. He was a god of regeneration, artisans and craftsmen, in particular stonemasons and may have originally been a fertility god. His connections with other gods include Seker (another crafts god) and Osiris, god of the underworld.

Ra (Re): Ra was a sun god closely connected with pharaoh. He was the head of the Ennead of Heliopolis. He was represented as a ram-headed man in a shrine, or a falcon with a sun disk. Other gods become associated with Ra in order to give them a solar aspect and to enhance their importance. Such as, Amun-Ra, Ra-Harakhte and Sobek-Ra. At the end of the day Ra was said to die and sail on a nightly voyage through the Underworld, leaving the moon to light the Earth. The boat would sail through the twelve doors, representing the twelve hours of night until he was reborn at dawn. However it was not always plain sailing as during his voyage Ra had to fight his main enemy, the snake god, Apep.

Satet (Satis): Satet was an archer-goddess of the Nile cataracts. Her name is often translated as 'She Who Shoots' (Arrows). She was a goddess of the hunt, fertility, inundation and guardian over the Nile cataracts. As a warrior goddess, she protected the pharaoh and the southern borders of ancient Egypt. Her most important role was as the goddess of the yearly Nile flood. According to myth, on the 'Night of the Teardrop' Satet would catch the single tear shed by Isis and poured it into the Nile, causing the inundation. By the New Kingdom era she was the wife of Khnum and the mother of Anuket, forming the Elephantine triad. She was worshiped throughout the Aswan area.

181

Sekhmet: This feline Egyptian goddess is known as the Eye of Ra and is the power that protects the good and annihilates the wicked. Sekhmet is a warrior god from Upper Egypt with leonine head, female human body and sun disk. She was depicted as a lioness, as it was the fiercest hunter known to the Egyptians. Sekhmet is a solar deity and is often associated with the goddesses Hathor and Bast. She was the goddess of retribution, vengeance, conquest and war but also the 'patron' of the Physicians, Priests and Healers. She is regarded as one of the most powerful of all the Gods. Her father was Ra and she inherited all his strength. She was worshipped principally at Memphis. Her name literally translated means Mighty One, or Powerful One. Sekhmet was the wife of Ptah and is undoubtedly one of the most ancient deities known to the human race.

Seth (Set, Sutekh): Son of Nut and Geb, brother of Isis and Osiris, brother and husband to Nephthys. He was known as the Red-God of the desert and thunderstorms. His animal representations were as a pig, donkey, hippo (see above) and an animal as yet unidentified that has a long dog-like body, stiff forked tail and square-topped ears. He is best known as the murderer of Osiris. However originally, as an ancient god, he was not considered wicked, but fell into this category during Egypt's long history. In fact Seti I took him as his god and for a time he became a favourite during that dynasty.

Shu: Was the god of air, light, the Guardian of the King, Supporter of the Heavens and the Son of Atum. He was popular in the New Kingdom and was usually associated with the sun god Ra. The main site of worship was at Naytabut, south east of Heliopolis. He was usually depicted as a lion, or as a man stood holding up Nut, his daughter, the sky goddess. He was said to give the 'Breath of Life' to all creatures.

 **Sobek (Suchos):** Sobek was an ancient god of crocodiles, first mentioned in the Pyramid Texts. He was known as the Lord of Fayum, and it is thought his worship originated in that area. The people of Egypt worshipped him to gain his protection and strength. He was a god of fertility and rebirth, and the symbolic strength of the ruler of Egypt. The word sovereign was written with the hieroglyph of a crocodile. It was thought Sobek could protect the Pharaoh from dark magic. Sobek can be depicted either as a crocodile-headed man or as a full crocodile and was worshipped wherever the River Nile presented difficulties, such as cataracts, fast flowing areas, swamp and marshland. He is usually shown holding a staff and ankh. Mummified crocodiles representing the god have been found in many ancient tombs in order to enlist his protection in the afterlife.

Taweret (Taurt, Greek –Thoeris):
The hippopotamus goddess with large sagging breasts who was the guardian of women in childbirth.

Tefnut: A lion-headed goddess who was the moisture in the air, the clouds in the sky and the dew on the ground. A primeval goddess borne out of the Ennead Heliopolis legend.

Thoth: A moon god who was the scribe of the gods. He was the inventor of writing and kept account of the years. He was highly regarded throughout Egypt, especially because of his

183

position of learning and intellect. He is depicted as a man with a head of the ibis bird.

EGYPTIAN TRIADS

A triad was a group of three main gods and goddesses that became associated with a particular temple. The divine triads represented the basic nuclear family of father, mother and son or daughter. Often the head of the Triad was one of the creator gods like Ptah, Khnum or Amun. Below are some of the temples and their adopted Triads.

ABYDOS:	Osiris, Isis and Horus
PHILAE:	Osiris, Isis and Horus
THEBES:(Karnak & Luxor)	Amun, Mut and Khonsu
MEMPHIS:	Ptah, Sekhmet and Nefertem
EDFU:	Horus, Hathor and Horsmatawy
ELEPHANTINE:	Khnum, Satet and Anuket
KOM OMBO: 1	Sobek, Hathor and Khonsu
KOM OMBO: 2	Horus, Tasenetnefret and Panebtawy

EGYPTIAN SYMBOLS

Ankh: Believed to unlock the mysteries of heaven and earth. Hence, the reason it is referred to as, 'The Key of Life'. The design appears to combine the symbolic cross of Osiris and the oval of Isis. It is often shown being carried by the gods and pharaoh.

Cartouche: Sign for Encircling Protection. In the form of a knotted rope it was used to enclose the royal name of the pharaoh. As with the Shen hieroglyph the cartouche signified the concept of surrounding protection. The cartouche may also have symbolised the universe being circled by the sun. Even the sarcophagi of some of the 18-19th dynasty pharaohs take on this shape and some tombs are also cartouche shaped, e.g. Tuthmoses III, affording the king that extra protection.

Crook (Sceptre): Symbol of Guardianship. The symbolism of the crook is similar to that of the stick and its derivatives, namely, power and authority. In ancient Egypt the royal symbol was called 'Heka' when it was in the shape of a shepherd's crook and a 'Was' when it had the head of a canine animal and a two-pronged base. The triple sceptre was made up of a whip, a staff and stick, representing domination over matter, control of feeling and domination of thought. It is a symbol of the central axis, like the king himself, the intermediary between god and his subjects, a guarantee of peace and justice. The royal symbol of the kings was adopted from the god Osiris and the ancient shepherd deity, Andjeti. It denoted Pharaoh's role as guardian of the People of the Nile. The crook and flail were used in all royal ceremonies and were part of the mortuary regalia of the kings, ensuring the continued welfare of the diseased in the Afterlife.

185

Djed Pillar: The symbol of Osiris, god of the Dead. In the book of the dead it is described as Osiris' backbone. It seems to have come to represent stability. Other gods that have been associated with it are Sokar and Ptah. It was at Memphis that the ceremony known as, '*raising the djed pillar*' was probably first carried out by Pharaoh, which represented the stability of the monarchy and the resurrection of Osiris. The best depiction of this act is in the Osiris Hall at Abydos.

Eye of Horus: Sign for Healing. During his confrontations with the god Seth, Horus is said to have lost his left eye, which represented the moon. However his wife, the goddess Hathor, restored it. That is why the *wedjat* (Eye of Horus) symbolises healing. Extremely common as an amulet it represented strength, protection, perfection, and the act of 'making whole'.

Flail: A symbol of Guardianship. The flail has long associations with the gods Osiris, Min, and several sacred animals. Like the crook, it was one of the important insignias of royalty. Some scholars believe it to be a whip, maybe derived from a fly-whisk. Whilst others think it represents the '*ladanisterion*', an instrument used by very early goat herders. As such, the flail would symbolise past traditions and the shepherding aspects of Pharaoh's role as king. The ancient Egyptian name for a flail was '*nekhakha*'.

Lotus: The sign for Rebirth and the emblem of Upper Egypt. Temple pillars often have lotus carved capitals. The lotus was symbolic of rebirth, since one of the creation myths describes how the newborn sun god rose out of a floating lotus. To celebrate this occurrence there was a hymn sung in the temple on festival days, the Lotus Offering, especially at the cult centre of Edfu. The blue lotus was also the emblem of the god Nefertem; 'The Lord of Perfume'. The lotus also appears to have been strongly connected with enjoyment and sensuality.

Obelisk: The word obelisk comes from the Greek word *obelos*, which means a pointed object. The Greeks in particular used the word to refer to the distinctive monuments of ancient Egypt. Obelisks were typically erected in pairs on the ceremonial way on either side of the entrance to a temple or tomb and it's thought that the monolith represented the primordial mound upon which the rays of the sun shone first. Egyptian obelisks were made from single blocks of red granite or similar rock, and the pyramidal top (pyramidion), most likely was sheathed in gold.

Pyramid: The pyramid is the symbol of Ascension. As a certain amount of astronomical observation was involved in the building of the pyramids, in particular the precise alignment with the cardinal points, it is believed the pyramid was a representation of the world's axis, with the body of the structure symbolising man's ascent to the heavenly skies - in particular, Pharaoh's ascension to Heaven and the Afterlife. It has also been proposed that the pyramid may have symbolised the sloping rays of the sun as a source of eternal strength and energy. Or it could have been designed to represent the Primeval Mound of Creation on which the sun-god was said to have been born.

Scarab: The sign of Resurrection. The scarab was a favourite amulet (charm) becoming associated with renewal and regeneration. It personified the god, Khepri, a sun god associated with resurrection. From the middle kingdom faineance scarabs were often used as a royal seal by pharaoh and would also be produced to celebrate certain events during his reign. There are various funerary types, for example, the large winged scarab and the heart scarab, which would be inserted within the linen wrapping during the mummification process.

Sphinx: The sign of Wisdom and Protection. With a human head, body of a beast, the sphinx had access to all wisdom and strength and symbolised the riddle of human existence.

187

USEFUL EGYPTIAN WORDS

1	wahed
2	etnien
3	talata
4	arbaa
5	khamsa
6	sitta
7	sabaa
8	thamania
9	tesaa
10	ashara
20	eshreen
21	wahed eshreen
22	etnien whe eshreen
50	khamsin
100	mia
500	khams mia
1000	elf

Airport mattar
Bathroom hammam
Beer beera
Big kabier
Beautiful gamil
Chicken dajaaj
Coffee ahua
Daughter bint
Doctor doctur
Eat yacol
Emergency tawarek
Fish samak
Food akal
Fork showka
Full maliin
God Willing inshaalha
Gold dahab
Goodbye ma'a'salam / Salam (peace)
Good Evening masa el-kheir
Good Morning sabah el-kheir
Good Night tesbah ala kheir
Go away imshe
How much? bekam
I don't understand ana mish fahem
I want ariyad or aawez
Is it far? hal bieat

It's Too Expensive ghali awi
knife sikkiyn
Leave me alone sebni fi haelee
Little shoeya
Long tawiel
Marketplace souk
Milk halib
Money feluus
Museum mat-hhaf
My name is ana ismee
Never mind maalish
No la (or la'a)
No, I don't have laa ma audich
No, thank you La'a shukran
Now delwakty
Open maftah
Outside barra
Pharmacy sighdaliya
Please min fadlak (male) min fadlik (Female)
Possible mumken
Restaurant mataam
Salt malh
Sleep noum
Slowly shwai
Sorry / Excuse me assef
Soup shurba
Station mahatta
Sugar sokkar
Thank you shukran
That's Fine/Perfect tamam
Tea shay
Telephone teliphune
Ticket tazkara
Town medina
Vegetables khudra
Water mayya
Welcome marhaba
What is this eh dah?
What do you call this in arabic? maza tosumi haza bel arabi?
Where fein
Where Can I Buy...? fein mumken ashtari...?
Wine nebite
Yes aywa,(Luxor) naam (Cairo)

HISTORY

The official language of Egypt is Egyptian Arabic. As the language of the Quran, the holy book of Islam, Arabic is widely understood throughout the Muslim world. Today over 200 million people speak Arabic and it is the official language of 18 countries. Some 90 million people speak Egyptian Arabic.

Arabic was originally the language of the nomadic Bedouin in the North Arabian Desert and has its origins in the Semitic language, which is closely related to Hebrew. The Arabic alphabet is believed to have evolved from that of an ancient people known as the Nabateans. Then, in the seventh century when the Muslims conquered much of the Middle East and North Africa, Arabic displaced the native language in many countries, including Coptic in Egypt.

STRUCTURE

The Arabic alphabet consists of 28 consonants and three vowels (a, i, u), which can be short or long. Some of the sounds are unique to Arabic and difficult for non-native speakers to pronounce correctly, though you should be able to make yourself understood.

Arabic sentences are usually written from right to left and the normal structure of a sentence is verb-subject-object. Nouns are inflected and marked for case, gender (masculine and feminine), number (singular, plural, dual and collective) and determination (definite and indefinite). Arabic has very few irregular verbs and does not use "is" or "are". For example 'busy the man' means 'the man is busy'.

MONEY CONVERSION CHART

The chart below should only be used as a rough guide as the exchange rate constantly alters. For example in January 2008 you would have received 10 Egyptian pounds to £1 sterling. However in June 2010 you would have only got 7LE to the pound. In October 2010 the going rate had improved to 8.8LE to the pound.

Before leaving for Egypt remember to check for current rates. You will find a currency converter on our website.

I've used the rate of **10LE to the £1** sterling in the chart below

EGYPT (LE)	UK (£)	US ($)	CANADA ($)	EUROPE (EURO)	AUSTRALIA ($)
1	0.10	0.18	0.21	0.15	0.25
5	0.50	0.90	1.05	0.75	1.25
10	1.00	1.80	2.10	1.50	2.50
15	1.50	2.70	3.15	2.25	3.75
20	2.00	3.60	4.20	3.00	5.00
35	3.50	6.30	7.35	5.25	8.75
50	5.00	9.00	10.50	7.50	12.50
75	7.50	13.50	15.75	11.25	18.75
100	10.00	18.00	21.00	15.00	25.00

Other Sterling Exchange Rates

7LE to the £1	8LE to the £1	9LE to the £1
1LE =14p	1LE =12.5p	1LE =11p
5LE =72p	5LE = 62.5p	5LE =55p
10LE =£1.42p	10LE = £1.25	10LE =£1.11
20LE = £2.86	20LE = £2.50	20LE = £2.22
50LE = £7.14	50LE = £6. 25	50LE = £5.55
100LE = £14.29	100LE = £12.50	100LE = £11.11

SPECIAL OFFERS

ETERNAL RIVER by STEVEN WOOD
Music to Sail the Nile By

Save on the Normal RRP of £8.99

Special Discount Only Available Through This Book

Use the link below to take advantage of this great discount

www.travel-egypt.co.uk/cd-offer.php

If you are looking for something special to listen to during your Egyptian holiday then I would suggest our 'Eternal River' music which is available for download from our website. The music is ideal for use with any mp3 player, iPod or to burn to your own CD. This Ancient Egyptian inspired music has been especially written for us and is presently only available from our websites, where you can listen to samples.

TRAVEL EGYPT SERIES: EBOOKS

Around Luxor and Photographing the Ancient Sites

Save on the Normal RRP with a Special Discount Price Only Available Through This Book

The above are the second and third books in the Travel Egypt series. Currently they are only available via our websites, as eBooks.

The 'Around Luxor' eBook explains what you can expect from a hotel-based holiday in Luxor. It covers many aspects including, bartering suggestions, medical advice, scams, accessibility, the best way to deal with hassle and advice on how to get around Luxor. It also covers the main shops, popular places to eat, toilets, markets, plus more general information regarding Luxor and the surrounding areas. The last section looks at some of the main hotels in Luxor which are regularly used by travel companies, showing wherever possible, exterior and interior shots. The eBook has been put together from our own photographic collection, experiences and personal observations.

The 'Photographing the Ancient Sites' eBook has been written for those of you on a package holiday with average photographic skills. Our aim when writing this book was to demonstrate what is possible with the most basic of camera equipment and technical know-how. Therefore the vast majority of photographs in the book have been chosen simply because they can be easily replicated by most people. Plus, we have also tried to keep the technical side of photography down to a bare minimum so that the information will be of use to the vast majority of readers. The book covers the main tourist sites and contains over 250 original photographs.

You can find our eBooks by using the link below
www.travel-egypt.co.uk/ebook-offer.php

*The author of this book reserves the right to withdraw this offer at anytime or change the URL link. If you would like to purchase our eBooks but find the link unavailable please contact us through our website.

ILLNESS AND MINOR ACCIDENT CLAIMS

The following is a guide as to what may be required in order to make a successful insurance claim.

1) Keep **ALL** original documents pertaining to your holiday, such as holiday brochure (or links to online web pages – add to favourites) that contain all the details of your holiday, including a copy of the terms and conditions at the time of booking and your insurance policy details.

2) As a matter of course keep a detailed diary of **ALL** your holiday events. For example;
   a) Welcome Meeting details (including rep's name for future reference)
   b) When, where and what you ate and drank
   c) When, where you went and what you did
   d) How you felt, what you saw.
   e) Anything that happened
   Keep the diary not only from the time of your illness but from day one, so you can easily recall events if asked to do so. Remember illness can have an incubation period so better to be prepared from the start.
   Most of the remaining points below will need to be written down in your diary should you fall ill or have an accident. If you are not capable of doing so, get your companion to do it for you.

3) Write down any illness or accident in full detail: dates, time, symptoms, location etc. (Record everything!)

4) Witnesses: Should you know of anyone else who is similarly ill or witnessed your illness or accident, then if they are willing, exchange contact details, name, cabin number, home address and telephone number as this would definitely help in the support of any claim.

5) If possible get your companion to video your illness. (e.g. sickness, sweating, pains) If you suffer an accident, video the injury as soon as possible and what caused it. (I realise, this is easier said than done)

6) If you need a doctor, record the visit in your diary. Making a note of the doctor's name, what was said and done, the medication prescribed and any fees charged. If you are given a prescription photograph it before having it filled out. Also if applicable should you or a companion go to the Chemist, note the name and address of the pharmacy, the cost of the medicines and obtain a receipt. If the doctor writes a report on your condition you should request a copy or at least have him inform you of what he has written. (e.g. what he thinks is the cause of your illness) Keep any medication packaging. (And photograph it as a backup). List out of pocket expenses; doctor's fees, taxis, medication, hospital costs, etc.

7) Tell your travel representative if you become ill (or have an accident) and get it officially recorded and make sure you get your own copy of the report signed by your rep. This is VERY important! The tour rep may or may not want to fill in an incident form at this time as they usually assume most illness is due to weak European stomachs, over exposure to the sun or over indulgence. However insist that it is recorded for your own peace of mind. A note about hotel or ship management: Many do not take kindly to you suggesting they have caused your illness or accident, and some on occasion have been known to become aggressive, therefore if at all possible avoid discussing the matter with them and talk only with your travel representative.

8) Write down any discussions you had with your rep and any action they took, (or didn't) in as much detail as you and your companion can remember.

9) Photograph any forms you fill in for your rep before handing them in.

10) Inconspicuously photograph and/or video anything that will support your case. If you are unable to do this, then at least make sure you write down any poor hygiene standards/practices you witness. Good evidence would include;
    o Poor hygiene stands; Kitchen staff not wearing gloves when handling food - filling bread basket, making fresh omelettes or stacking pancakes. Restaurant staff with dirty uniforms. I observed a chef in the restaurant with a freshly blood stained apron due to a cut on his wrist that hadn't been bandaged properly.
    o Dirty facilities such as rooms, bathrooms, toilets and pools. We experienced a toilet that pooled dirty water on the bathroom floor every time it was flushed.

11) For those of you involved in accidents, discreetly photograph or video the cause of your injury, plus accidents waiting to happen such as broken steps, rocks, things left lying around, exposed cable, piping, trip hazards etc. If you are unable to photograph, then at least write down the details including the name of the place where you were at the time.

12) If you have to report anything to reception make a note of the date, time and who you spoke to. For example; your electricity goes off, or your shower is leaking.

13) Keep **ALL** receipts; Bills / Tickets / Bookings. (E.g. meals, medicine, doctors, pharmacy, taxis, purchases, excursions etc.) They will all help to prove where you were and what you did. You may have to ask for a receipt as Egyptians are not very forthcoming with them. Some will probably refuse to provide them, for example taxi drivers – just note in your diary the cost for future reference.

14) Keep any texts you send to family and friends, as evidence of events. Also keep their replies.
15) Depending on whom you have booked with you may be asked to fill out a form either at your departure meeting or on the flight back home regarding the service you have received. If possible I suggest you photograph this prior to handing it in, as negative responses have been known to go missing.
16) Upon your return visit your own doctor as soon as possible. You will be asked to provide a stool sample. Tell your doctor **ALL** the symptoms you've experienced so they are officially recorded. (Solicitors from both sides will refer to your medical records.) Do not leave it too long before your visit. Pain and suffering does come into the equation when a settlement fee is discussed.
17) Continue with your diary even when you get home, listing ongoing symptoms, appointments and other problems, such as; time off work, lost wages.
18) Contact your travel insurance to see if you are covered. If not, check out any other insurance policies you may have (e.g. home, work, union).
19) If you do issue a claim, keep all documentation listed above until your case is settled one way or another. Including any letters / forms you've completed regarding your claim since your return home.

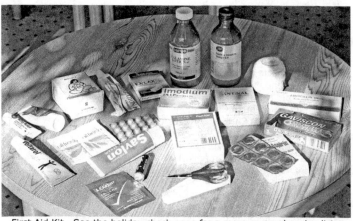

First Aid Kit. See the holiday check page for a more comprehensive list.

BIBLIOGRAPHY
In no particular order
Used for historical information on our website, books and eBooks

BOOK REFERENCE:
A Concise Dictionary of Egyptian Archaeology: Brodrick & Morton
The Arts and Crafts of Ancient Egypt: Flinders Petrie
Akhenaton's Egypt: Angela P Thomas
Egyptian Household Animals: Rosalind and Jac J Jenssen
Getting Old in Ancient Egypt: Rosalind and Jac J Jenssen
Egypt: Land of the Pharaohs: Lost Civilisations (Publisher)
Egyptian Mythology: Simon Goodenough
Monuments of Civilisation: Egypt: Claudio Barocus
A-Z of Mythology: Peter Clayton
The Illustrated Encyclopaedia Of Animal Life: Odhams (Publisher)
The Ancient World: Hamlyn (Publisher)
A Pictorial History of the Talkies: (Revised)John Kobal Spring Books
Film Review (s): Edited by F Maurice Speed (publisher MacDonald)
Romance and the Cinema: John Kobal
A Thousand and One Delights: Alan G Barbour
A Pictorial History of Film Musicals: John Kobal
Cinema Preview: Edited by Eric Warman
The Greatest Movie Stars (International Years): David Shipman
Egypt. The World of the Pharaohs: Konemann (Publishers)
Cleopatra's Palace. In search of a Legend: Laura Foreman
Ancient Egypt: Lorna Oakes and Lucia Gahlin
Egypt - Gods, Myths and Religion: Lucia Gahlin
Daughters of Isis: Joyce Tyldesley
Egypt - The Rough Guide (Publisher)
Gods of Ancient Egypt: Barbara Watterson
Life in Egypt in Ancient Times: Bernard Romant
The Penguin Historical Atlas of Ancient Egypt: Bill Manley
What Life was Like on the Banks of the Nile: Time Life Books
Myth and Legends of Egypt: Lewis Spence
Ancient Egypt: Myth and History: Geddes and Grosset (Publisher)
A Dictionary of Egyptian Civilisation: Georges Posener
Egypt: Robertson McCarta and Nelles Verlag
Egyptian Language: Sir E A Wallis Budge
The Search for Ancient Egypt: New Horizons (Publisher)
The Secret Language of Symbols: David Fontana
The Mammoth Dictionary of Symbols: Nadia Julian
Gods of Eden: Andrew Collins
Egypt Before the Pharaohs : Michael A Hoffman
Egyptian Grammar: Sir Alan Gardiner
Understanding Hieroglyphs: Hilary Wilson
British Museum Dictionary of Ancient Egypt: Ian Shaw
Guide to the Valley of the Kings: Alberto Siliotti
The Pyramids: Aberto Siliotti
Growing up in Ancient Egypt: Rosalind M and Jac J Janssen
Akhenaton: king of Egypt: Cyril Aldred
Egyptian Warfare and Weapons: Ian Shaw
Sexual Life in Ancient Egypt: Lise Manniche

Family Life in Ancient Egypt: Peter Clayton
Egyptians: Rachel Wright
Great Civilisations: Micropedia (Publisher)
The Penguin Atlas Of Ancient History: Colin McEvedy
The Book of the Dead: Sir E A Wallis Budge
Magic and Mystery in Ancient Egypt: Christian Jacq
Valley of the Kings: John Romer
Egyptian Mummies: Bob Brier
Egyptian Mummies: Barbara Adams
Growing up in Ancient Egypt: Rosalie David
Lonely Planet: Egyptian Arabic Phrasebook
BBC Travel Pack : Arabic
The Mummy: Joyce Tyldesley
People of the Pharaohs: Hilary Wilson
Egypt under the Pharaohs: Heinrick Brugsch-Bey
The Splendour that was Egypt: Margaret A Murray
The Egyptians: Michael Hayes
Ancient Egypt in Nineteenth Century Paintings: Berko
The Rape of the Nile: Brian M Fagan
The Egyptians: Cyril Aldred
Women in Ancient Egypt: Barbara Watterson
The Hermetica: Timothy Freke and Peter Gandy
The Encyclopaedia of Ancient Egypt: Margaret Bunson
Egyptian Life: Miriam Stead

INTERNET REFERENCES:
http://www.bbc.co.uk
http://www.cnn.com/
http://www.fco.gov.uk
http://travel.state.gov/
http://abcnews.go.com/
http://www.reuters.com
http://english.aljazeera.net/
http://www-wds.worldbank.org/
http://en.wikipedia.org/
http://www.ancientegypt.co.uk/
http://www.soundandlight.com.eg/
http://weekly.ahram.org.eg/
http://www.youtube.com/
http://www.thebanmappingproject.com/
http://www.irinnews.org/
http://www.almasryalyoum.com/en
http://news.egypt.com/
http://wwwnc.cdc.gov/travel/destinations/egypt.aspx
http://www.thebrooke.org/

ACKNOWLEDGEMENT:
I would like to give special thanks to all of those readers who contacted
me with their stories and information after reading our first edition.
Your input was much appreciated.

LISTS OF TERRORIST ATTACKS AND ACCIDENTS

The following lists are provided for those of you wanting more information regarding events of terrorism and major accidents that have happened in Egypt. However please bear in mind that the chances of anything happening to you are extremely unlikely. Over 12 million people visited Egypt last year (2010) and it has to be said that the vast majority of tourists find their experience hugely enjoyable and trouble free.

The information below is not included to instil needless anxiety, but given so you can study the issue of personal safety in Egypt before making an informed decision about whether to travel to this beautiful but sometimes troubled region.

In order to put things into perspective, ensure you consider the dates when reading this information.

TERRORIST ATTACKS

- 2010: On December 31st a terrorist car bomb exploded occurred outside a Christian church in Egypt's northern city of Alexandria which killed seven people and wounded 24 others, including eight Muslims. Egypt has a large Christian minority, who make up about 10 percent of the population. The rest of the country is Muslim. This is not the first clash between the differing religions this year. In November 2010 a confrontation between hundreds of Christians and riot police in Cairo took a sectarian turn when dozens of Muslims became involved in the violence as the Christians protested against the decision to halt construction of a church in a Cairo suburb. One Christian was killed and dozens were hurt in the scuffles. These attacks were not aimed at tourists.

- 2010: On 6th January around seven people were killed in a drive-by shooting outside a church in Naj Hammadi in southern Egypt. This attack was not aimed at tourists.

- 2009: On February 22nd a terrorist bomb killed a French teenager and wounded at least 20 other people in a crowded square near a popular tourist bazaar in Cairo. The bomb exploded near the 14th-century Khan el-Khalili market where holiday-makers shop for small gifts and relax at outdoor cafes. So this latest deadly attack was clearly aimed at foreign tourists. The injured included French, German, Saudi and Egyptian. The bomb exploded under a bench in a garden in the square.

- 2008: On 22nd September 19 European tourists, including Germans, Italians and one Romanian, and eight Egyptians were abducted in the Egyptian desert from a safari tour conducted near Egypt's south-western borders with Sudan and Libya. The kidnappers then rushed their captives southward into the harsh desert terrain of Sudan and demanded a multi-million-dollar ransom. Their freedom came when military forces swarmed their camp, killing several of the terrorists in the process. All 19 hostages were freed unharmed.

- 2006: April 24th three bombs exploded in the bustling Egyptian Sinai seaside resort of Dahab, killing 23, mostly Egyptians, but also a German, Lebanese, Russian, Swiss and a Hungarian. At least 80 people were wounded including tourists from Australia, Denmark, France, Germany, Israel, Lebanon, Palestine, South Korea, United Kingdom and the United States. Investigations revealed the blasts were suicide attacks, set off by Bedouins.
- 2005: On 23rd July a number of bombs exploded in the vibrant resort town of Sharm el-Sheikh when more than 200 people were injured and 88 were killed from at least 5 different countries.
- 2005: Another two attacks on tourists in Cairo happened at the end of April when 3 persons were killed and 7 people were injured. The first attack involved a man who jumped from a bridge during a police chase and ignited a bomb he was carrying, killing himself. The second incident involved two veiled women in there twenties when they opened fire on a tour bus in a historic district of Cairo, wounding two passengers before killing themselves. The authorities ascertained the first bomber was the brother and fiancé of two women who attacked the bus. These incidents occurred behind the Egyptian Museum. Four of the wounded were foreign tourists. A group calling itself the Abdullah Azzam Brigades claimed responsibility.
- 2005: On the 7th April near the Khan El Khalili bazaar, 3 tourists were killed and 19 people injured when a suicide bomber belonging to a fringe extremist group delivered a crude homemade bomb, packed with nails, on the back of a motorcycle, right into the heart of the historic shopping bazaar called Khan al-Khalili. The blast killed 2 tourists, a French woman and an American man, and wounded about 18 other people, some critically. The terrorist was also killed.
- 2004: There were three terrorist attacks on the 7th October at Taba and Nuweiba when 34 people were killed (including tourists) and 159 injured.
- 1997: Egypt's tourism industry was crippled after the November attack by Islamic fundamentalist that left fifty eight foreign tourists and four Egyptians dead in Luxor at Hatshepsut's Temple. (Deir el-Bahri) Six of the attackers and three policemen were amongst the dead in the violence.
- 1996: On 18th April terrorists carried out the mass murder of 18 Greeks at a bus shelter near the pyramids where 150 were waiting for a coach. Apparently they were mistaken for Israelis.

- 1994: November 6th Gunmen opened fire at a Nile cruiser carrying 30 tourists in southern Egypt, but did not cause any damage or casualties.
- 1994: A British tourist is killed and three others wounded in an attack on a minibus on 23rd October.
- 1994: On the 27th September a German is killed and another wounded during an attack at the Red Sea resort of Hurghada. Two Egyptians were also killed. The injured German died of his wounds after returning home.
- 1994: On the 26th August a Spanish boy is killed in an attack on a tourist bus in southern Egypt.
- 1994: March 13th Gunmen fired at a Nile cruiser in southern Egypt, but no one was hurt.
- 1994: March 4th gunmen fired at a Nile cruiser in southern Egypt, wounding a German woman tourist, who died after being flown back to Germany.
- 1994: February 17th gunmen opened fire on a Nile cruiser in Assiut, but no one is hurt.
- 1993: On the 27 October a mentally unstable man described as a musician shoots dead two US businessmen, a French tourist and an Italian at a luxury Cairo hotel.
- 1993: On September 15th and 18th Muslim militants fired at two Nile cruise boats, the first near the village of al-Qusiya, the second on a boat carrying 22 French tourists near Abu Tig, in Upper Egypt. Both attacks missed and no one was hurt.
- 1993: August 16th a lone gunman fired shots at a tourist boat in southern Egypt, but nobody is hurt.
- 1993: 8 June 1993: A blast near a tour bus on the pyramids Road in Cairo kills two Egyptians and wounds 22 others, including five Britons.
- 1993: On the 26th February a bomb went off in a crowded coffee shop in central Cairo killing a Turk, Swede and Egyptian. 20 other people were wounded.
- 1992: On the 21st October a British woman is killed and two British men wounded in an attack near Dairut in the south of the country. The woman was the first foreigner to die in Egypt due to a terrorist attack.
- 1992: On the 1st October the first terrorist attack by Islamic militants on tourists took place when gunmen opened fire on a cruise boat carrying 140 Germans. Several Egyptian crew members were injured.

FATAL ROAD ACCIDENTS

- December 2010: Eight American tourists were killed and 21 injured when their coach hit a stationary truck in southern Egypt. The bus, which was carrying 37 tourists from the United States, was headed to the ancient Egyptian Abu

200

Simbel temples when it hit a damaged truck parked on the side of the road. Officials said six of the dead were women. The crash occurred early in the morning about 19 miles from Aswan. Four tourists were in critical condition with some of the wounded, being airlifted to a hospital in Cairo that often treats injured tourists.

- November 2010: Eight tourists were killed and more than 22 others injured in a bus crash on the highway between Cairo and Hurghada. Apparently the driver lost control of the vehicle which turned over. The victims were Russians, Ukrainians, Germans, Belgian and Egyptians.
- October 2010: A German woman died in a car accident in the Sinai Peninsula.
- October 2010: One Italian tourist was killed when the bus she was travelling on overturned on a main road in the Red Sea resort of Sharm el-Sheikh. Two Germans, one Italian and a Japanese tourist were injured, along with the Egyptian driver.
- January 2010: Eighteen French tourists were injured when their bus overturned on the two-lane desert road to Abu Simbel.
- May 2008: Nine people were killed and 28 injured after a tourist bus crashed and caught fire in Egypt's Sinai Peninsula. The bus apparently rounded a sharp bend and overturned. Russians, Egyptians, Britons, Canadians, Italians, Romanians and Ukrainians were among the casualties, with many badly burned.
- February 2008: At least 29 people were killed and 16 injured when a bus, nine cars and several lorries slammed into each other on a fog-choked rural highway in Upper Egypt.
- December 2005: Twenty-one Egyptians were killed and 33 injured in two separate road accidents south of Cairo. A collision between a minibus and a lorry killed 16 people and injured seven. Whilst five others were killed and 26 hurt when a coach heading from Cairo to the Red Sea resort of Hurghada overturned when its front tyre burst.
- August 2003: A horrific road crash that happened near the Egyptian city of Minya left 21 people dead and 39 injured when a bus burst into flames after it was in collision with a van and flipped over. It's believed the driver of the bus may have dozed off behind the wheel. Five children are among the dead, two of whom were babies. Most of the dead were burnt alive.

INCIDENTS ON THE RIVER

- 2010: A British tourist was killed when a felucca capsized in bad weather on the Nile. The holidaymaker was with three others when their boat overturned in the southern city of Aswan in heavy winds and waves. It's reported that the sudden storm caused the boat to overturn. The boat had been booked as a two-day cruise along the Nile, and the tourists were sleeping on the craft.

- 2010: A Cruise ship crashes on the Nile River with another boat, port side. The collision caused people to be thrown off their seats and windows smashed. Passengers complained that they did not receive any safety briefing from the crew or their travel rep and were kept in the dark as to the severity of the collision. Fortunately no one was thrown overboard or injured by the impact.

- 2009: Two passenger ferries collided in the Nile Delta north of the Egyptian capital. Everyone was accounted for. At least a dozen injured people were taken to hospital.

- 2007: Five Egyptians were killed on 2nd December in a fire that broke out on a Nile cruise boat in Luxor. 43 French tourists were quickly evacuated from the three-storey boat after the fire broke out in the engine room overnight and quickly spread. No tourists were hurt. The five Egyptians who died were either trapped by flames as they tried to extinguish the blaze or drowned after falling into the river.

- 2003: On Wednesday, 15th October, a fire broke out on the Kempinski Ganna Nile Cruise Ship as it sailed from Luxor to Aswan near the port of Edfu. There were 144 passengers on board, 102 Spanish and 42 Italians. The fire rapidly got out of control and the Captain ordered the ship to be evacuated. Nearby boats enabled most passengers and crew to be off-loaded swiftly and safely. The Captain and the crew checked the ship before abandoning it themselves. Two injured passengers had to be transferred to a hospital in Luxor for further treatment, a 38-year old Spanish man suffering from burns and a 50-year old Spanish woman with a fractured arm. Nine other passengers suffered minor cuts and burns but they were quickly discharged from the local hospital. The Egyptian-owned ship, launched late in 2002 as a brand-new build had all the latest fire and safety equipment installed to meet the highest international standards. Although the cause of the fire is not yet confirmed, it is thought that it broke out in a passenger cabin. Evacuation procedures were followed properly and without panic, which prevented any more serious injuries occurring.

- 1996: At least six Czech and Slovak tourists and up to 18 Egyptian crew members were missing after a Nile cruise boat listed and took on water. The boat was carrying more than 70 Czechs and Slovaks between the tourist resorts of Aswan and Luxor.

FATAL RAIL INCIDENTS
(None involving tourists)

- October 2009: At least 18 people were killed in a collision between two trains on the outskirts of the Egyptian capital, Cairo. Another 36 were wounded. The trains were travelling on the same track. One ran into the other after the first train stopped when it hit a cow and 10 minutes later the second train arrived at full speed.

- July 2008: At least 37 people died and some 40 injured in a collision between a train and several vehicles at a level crossing in northern Egypt. The crash happened near Marsa Matruh, 430km (270 miles) northwest of the capital Cairo when a truck failed to stop at the crossing and pushed several waiting vehicles into the path of the oncoming train.

- February 2002: Over 370 people died and over 65 were injured whilst travelling from Cairo to Luxor. The authorities say it was caused by a fire started by a passenger and was not a crash. All the dead were Egyptian. It was Egypt's worst train disaster in 150 years.

- November 1999: Ten people are killed and seven injured when a train, travelling between Cairo and Alexandria, hit a truck and derailed.

- April 1999: A head on collision between trains in northern Egypt kills 10 people and nearly 50 are left injured.

- October 1998: Around 50 people are killed and over 80 injured in a derailment just south of Alexandria. The train failed to stop at the buffers and ploughed into a busy market square. It's thought that passengers travelling on the roof of the train may have tampered with an air pipe which disabled the brakes.

- February 1997: At least 11 people die after a collision caused by human error and a signalling failure north of Aswan.

- February 1996: A train hits a truck on a level crossing 90 kilometres north of Cairo, killing 11 people.

- December 1995: A train rams into the back of another in thick fog, killing 75 people. The driver was blamed after it was found that the train was travelling above the national speed limit.

- May 1995: A train hits a barrier just north of Cairo and derails. Nine people die.

- April 1995: A train and a bus collide on a level crossing in the Nile Delta region, killing 49.

- December 1993: At least 12 people die and 60 are injured when two trains collide head on about 90 kilometres north of Cairo.

- February 1992: A head-on train collision just outside Cairo kills 43 people.

FATAL AIR ACCIDENTS
- 2007: In December an Italian tourist was slightly injured when a charter plane bound for the Egyptian Red Sea resort town of Sharm el-Sheikh made an emergency landing in Cairo after the cockpit windshield splintered.
- 2004: An Egyptian charter plane crashed into the Red Sea, killing all 148 passengers and crew on board. It went down shortly after leaving the Egyptian resort of Sharm el-Sheikh. Most of the passengers were French tourists, including many children, returning from holiday to Charles de Gaulle airport in Paris. French and Egyptian officials believe the crash was caused by technical failure.
- 2002: An EgyptAir Flight crashed into terrain in heavy rain, fog, and a sandstorm on its approach to Tunis, killing 15 of the 64 occupants.

RED SEA INCIDENTS
- 30th November 2010: A couple were badly mauled and suffered serious leg and back injuries after a shark attack.
- 1st December 2010: Four holiday makers were attacked by a shark at the popular Red Sea resort of Sharm el-Sheikh. Two Russian tourists had their arms bitten off as they swam. The beaches were temporarily closed. It's believed a single oceanic white tip shark was responsible for all four attacks.
- 3rd December 2010: Two sharks were caught, an Oceanic White Tip and a Mako and the beaches were reopened by officials.
- 5th December 2010: A German female tourist was killed by a shark while swimming off Egypt's Red Sea resort of Sharm el-Sheikh. The 70-year-old woman was the fifth person to be attacked. Holidaymakers were appalled that tourists were not warned, saying, even an hour after the attack people were still swimming, unaware of the danger. All water-sports and diving activities were closed at the resort.

- 26 February 2010: A luxury cruise liner crashed into a dock at the Egyptian Red Sea resort of Sharm-el-Sheikh killing 3 crew members and injuring at least 4 tourists. The Costa Europa was carrying 1,473 passengers and was coming into the harbour in bad weather. The injured reportedly included three British women and an Italian man.

INDEX